THE TREES
ARE STILL
BENDING
SOUTH

The Trees are Still Bending South © Sharron Proulx-Turner, 2012

Published by Kegedonce Press
11 Park Road, Cape Croker Reserve
R. R. 5, Wiarton, Ontario, N0H 2T0
www.kegedonce.com
Administration Office/Book Orders
RR7 Owen Sound, ON N4K 6V5

Copyeditor: Kateri Akiwenzie-Damm
Design: Red Willow Designs

Library and Archives Canada Cataloguing in Publication

Proulx-Turner, Sharron
    The trees are still bending south / Sharron Proulx-Turner.

Poems.
ISBN 978-0-9868740-2-4

    I. Title.

PS8581.R68983T74 2011   C811'.6   C2011-905937-1

Sales and Distribution - http://www.lpg.ca/LitDistco:
For Customer Service/Orders
Tel 1-800-591-6250 Fax 1-800-591-6251
100 Armstrong Ave. Georgetown, ON L7G 5S4
Email orders@litdistco.ca

Kegedonce Press gratefully acknowledges the generous support of:

 ONTARIO ARTS COUNCIL
CONSEIL DES ARTS DE L'ONTARIO

*We acknowledge the support of the Canada Council for the Arts which last
year invested $20.1 million in writing and publishing throughout Canada.*

 Canada Council   Conseil des Arts
for the Arts   du Canada

CONTENTS

THE HAZARDS OF 50S LOVE

IN THE FACE OF WATER

ACKNOWLEDGMENTS

this one's for you, aunty
Evelyn Thenola Rose-Ann Boyce
my rock
my inside-outside mom

my people will sleep for one hundred years.
when they awake, it will be the artists that
give them back their spirit.

louis riel

TRADITION CALLS FOR OUR RETURN

stories give us memory

tobacco on the water's blue
speaks a language shared by the ancients
mirrored there
the songs of many birds, hollowed out
from the centre of a great white pine
reaching out her arms, greens holding
winter's edge
her song the sound of earth

that same white pine
shows her mysteries
eyes turned inward
sees the water bird, the melting surface
of the lake
blend into the horizon

the lake, too
is looking inward
life revealing
holes in the ice
their roundness a looking glass
magnifying the water below

reaching for edges
of sand
touching footprints left behind
by a woman
ajinjagaayohn, giver of life

bear walker

if you were to help your fellow anishinauback, or your fellow human beings generally, what you must do is already set. however you may hate it, however unpleasant it may be, you must work at it. it is not always beautiful. and this – everything on the surface of the water is beautiful. to get to the source of beauty you must dig deep.
frank shawbedees and *basil johnston*

I like my tea strong and hot
but I drink it for the peace
and comfort tea brings
says my aunty
the burn on her hand from the oven
still red and raw
listen carefully, you, she says
and I'll tell you what I know
you look tired, I say
oh you, she winks at the moon
I'll sleep when I'm dead
there's times where I doubt
that I'm blessed, she says, but today
today is not one of those days

today I saw a cardinal
what a treat
last time I heard a cardinal's red, red song
I was a very little girl
about the time I lost my family
called my own mother mom
but I never knew her, eh
on account of the system
stole me from my home

I never confronted the old lady who raised me
on all her evil ways, her home-spun torture
of little girls, beaten and tossed around

like a rag doll, thrown against the wall
dead chicken tied around my neck for being bad
or lowered in the well, tied to a chair
who knows how long
last in the weekly bath
after eleven others washed themselves, same water, eh
no blankets or pillow to sleep with
so cold and my wet, still dirty, stinky hair
don't even remember most of those years
but what can you do when you live in a shoe

what I wanted to tell you today, my girl
is all my life I've dreamed of bear
like this one this morning, eh
where three grown, large she-bears
come up and out through the hot, brown sand of the ottawa
enter into a place I'm staying at
at ceremony, half in, half out of the sandy ground
beautiful dream, that, but never been to
a indian ceremony in my life, me
thanks to the government laws
that denied our old people their rights
denied us métis our place in this land

it was a world where sand unwinds every thought, that dream
every hope, trees growing out from that sand
out from that dream, like roots pull water
from under the ground, down to the centre of the earth
the hills of sand in that there dream
reflected the moon, her sharing that knowledge
inside each tiny grain

ain't I getting philosophical in my old age, me
but I seen a path in that there sand
the years folded in on themselves, backwards in time
all them people I helped at that place I worked
the years and years of putting in nights
with them folks no one wants to be around
no one wants them in their world, eh
some who can't remember their names
some who can't keep a tune
some who can't walk or eat or play
all them called crazy or nuts or worse
nicest folks you ever could know, them
they don't judge or berate or harm a pea
so many nights I loved it there, resented them too
their loose hold on this world, their rotten, dirty diapers
them hovering around the pills I put in them little cups
their whine, whine, whine
now I miss them sometimes, eh

but what I got to tell you today, my girl
the hem of my pant legs holds that sand now, eh
look here and see
I've been walking that sand around my ankles
dumping it onto the bathroom floor
here in this big city
me on this couch and you over there on that chair
I got some here in this tupperware
so you can keep it, you
seen words tumbling there, their warm, brown letters
like clothes swishing around in a wringer washing machine

then one of them bears folded into the shape of my body
in that dream
my tired, sad bones flying out from that bear
and onto the sand at my four brown feet

then me, I walked away from myself
my past, my life short as an ad on that there tv
and you know how much I love my tv, you
this sand comes from over there, eh
wherever over there is anyway
somehow, some way, they did this miracle here today
them bears

pay attention to your dreams, my girl
live your life like today's your first day
on this here earth
smile at people on the street, show your teeth, you
put this sand in a special place, keep it safe
when you put some in your warm, living hands, remember me
remember bear
and remember, when you think you can't outlive some pain
it's only honesty will help you survive
we're here to learn how to be human, us
and only humans can change who we are
but that change can shake, shake, shake us up, all right
like a bear at a tree on a hot summer night

please keep walking

signs on bridges
signs on roads
passing trucks pushing red
from the sides of their painted bodies
into my brain

same bus ride to ottawa
same roads and same houses
fifty years
fences hug the highway
clothes dry on a line

same worn-down pee stop
between what might be canada's largest city
and canada's capital
the city that hides behind its small
unfriendly airport
its greyhound station peeking out

from the depths of an old forest
where birds walked
their footprints become stars
an old forest, whose life, whose trees
long since downed and slaughtered
still long for home

same winds' hands
stretch outward
touch the ancient roots
that keep pulling me back
to the land of the pines
know the medicine that waits
to meet my skin
blue beneath the moon

inside the depths
my body's dark water
listens so hard
accelerated by sound bites and carbons
weaned on a post-contact rush
for capital gains and an insatiable need
for more

the fire's flame
leans my way
whispers
who could believe there is such a thing
as a song with the power
to hurt or kill
or a song that would
keep the world alive

out of the corner of my eye

you can tell a lot about a person
by how they treat their eagle feathers
when they're helping others
said a gifted algonquin warrior woman
some treat their eagle feathers
rough, hit hard with them
shake them feathers
till they're tattered and ruined
that door shut tight
against the helpers
on the other side

others feed their feathers
smudge them, care for them
hang them on a wall
treat them real gentle
when they help others

eagle feathers are gifts, eh
direct from the other side
they're here to teach us
how to treat our children
them eagle feathers are

treat our children real gentle
don't shake them, hit them
hurt them in any way

our children are
our greatest teachers
in this life
direct from the other side

it's the children we're to
always keep in our thoughts

their safety, their survival
the children choose us as parents
aunties uncles cousins grandparents friends
not the other way around

this is not a lecture, not a modern-day speech
but a story who knows us
remembers who we are
a story who knows how to protect
how to heal

the stories are alive, choose us
not the other way around
the stories are our ancestors
join with us in our time
love us, care for us
speak through us, eh
though we may not know this
at the time

my mother's name was jeanne d'arc

when I was young, I saw
through my mother's eyes
where black and white was
more than sixties tv
more than a photograph
of all us girls

under the christmas tree
I grew up next to water
the delicate fingers of white pine
backdropped by black bruises
around my mother's heart
her memories, a thousand storms

solid in her wake
she would say, my mother
that everything, our words
our thoughts, even our intent
travels by air, et moi
she would say, I have a strong

wind here inside me
her hand at her heart
beating to the rhythm
of trees and grasses
blowing upward there through
the night sky, out to the ancestors
the star sisters, the saints up there

on high, like jeanne d'arc
she'd say, now there was a girl
who saw out the heart's eye
and her but just a child
led an army, that one
scared the king so bad

her rule, her voice a wind with eyes
but frightened men are distant lands

their seas fed by women's blood
women's wombs, giants dwarfed
only by marriage or death or deed

so remember, girls, to hide
your knowing eyes, beneath
the sleepy ground, rest there
on our mother, the earth
for deep in her centre, that heat
that fire there is our teacher

wakes up a woman's mysteries, that fire
and mystery is power
the monarch butterflies come from there, them
their orange mirrored on the jewelweed
their blacks and whites the ashes of our lives
it's monarchs got us up off all fours

taught us how to walk
dreamed I was a monarch once
taught me
knowing can be a sad thing
for us girls, our skin like
butterfly wings

awake with rivers, streams
marshes, running through our blood
at moontime, when we bear down too
so stay awake, my girls
because in my day they kept us sleeping
while we birthed our babes

and sometimes we just stayed asleep for years
be like the owl, there, fly silent
hunt in that early evening light
like spider when she weaves her web
embroider us, stitch by stitch
take back our women's line

just as prayers are sometimes one-sided

this is a true story
my mom's first cousin, he's a priest
catholic, eh, urban, helps youth at risk
for forty years, fears for his life
so our mother, the earth, he says
is really our mother, the church
all smiles and floating up to the top
his gaze brown as molasses
on thick french toast
you confuse me, uncle, I say
I want to stuff those words
back into your mouth
give you tea instead of beer
but it 's like holding a wolf down by an ear

uncle's scapular, that picture thing he wears
around his neck, it shines in the dark
during the day it's just jesus being sad
but at night, that jesus comes to life
lights up in song
once I heard him sing, *the rose*
in three part harmony
not uncle singing, jesus, eh

one time my uncle died, for real
minutes on end
it's after that he starts to drink
it's after that his scapular starts to sing
even songs like, *I shot the sheriff*
jesus was a capricorn
the red river jig

uncle says he was murdered
(himself, not jesus)
that's how he died before he was revived

stabbed with a knife so many times
lost so much blood, the body and blood of christ
but his scapular stayed right clean, eh
all turquoise and brown, bit of white
stood out against his dying, black robes

when he died, he says he saw a world, eh
one of them after death experiences
nothing like in heaven, no moniyaw god the father
no white beard, no throne, no gold or jewels
no god at all, just his relatives, his bishop
his old red car, a opitisaskawin, a métis feast
he was still wearing his scapular over there, eh

kept him grounded, kept him mother earth bound
there's lots more, he tells me when he's in the drink
wrote it all down in a book
lays that book in a safe deposit box, indian bank
with the tenderness of a saint

don't let this book out till I die, my girl, eh
they'd kick me out of the church
and I'm too old for that, me and jesus both
what happened, uncle, I ask him
I ask jesus too, at night when he's happy
singing, *god save the queen*

but uncle, he won't tell me, see
it's only kindness matters is what he says
as jesus breaks into that song sung by jewel
that's all youse need to know, eh
know love, love life, love, my girl, love
just love, jesus sings, *jesus christ, superstar*
the beatles', *love, love, love*
eyes gazing up at the starry, starry night

dis is a living english prefix

there are amazon women, recognized as such, *today* in a number of
tribes – young, alive, and kicking!

paula gunn allen

dis is not a tall tale, I tell her
a physician friend tells me
us women, we have thirty-two love-making glands
the men have something like two
so without dispute
we squirt thirty times more than any man

don't you think that's over
the top, she says
me I don't go there, orgasm creates discord
a disembodied, overrated state
like a woman's moontime
when the heart and mind
hold such distrust
a woman's love, her juices
not the path my life will take

dis is not a tall tale, I tell her
full moon out from the downpour
out from the storm
many old people hold moonstones
they're sacred those
even through the smells of woman love
patches of snow still hug the north sides of
moon lit hills, shiver in the shadow
of a grandmother's power
to shapeshift, to travel great distances
past and present, careful
not to disturb the lining of mother earth's womb

rebirthing a time when a small white butterfly
could hold a thousand words
up to a woman's flower
her power emerging
dissolving the pain there, reaching out
to shame, deep within our bellies
disturbing new roots whose eyes, awake now
look out from under the sand

the one shaped like a winter leaf

inside the low, long love-sounds
of wild turkeys
I see the edges of my own life
an ancient comb made from bone
I stand on a bed of pine needles
their bronzes reflected on my skin

summoned by the stories
that find their way into my fingers
behind my eyes
moving around inside me
changing my view of the world

a story on the news today
things european will fade away
from the americas
2030 and the white man
will be a minority on this land
history's sacred text
complementing itself
touching us all

scientists thought
the smartest people were those
who could distinguish the most of
forty thousand colour hues
their story quick to shift
the bullets didn't match the gun

white men could see
one thousand two hundred hues
white women four thousand
indigenous women
more than sixteen thousand

the browns of that
ride into the future
where the night sky beckons
with the silence that rests
after an orchestra performs
into the early hours

a round dance
a night ceremony, a yuwipi
an old man at a shaking tent ceremony
a road man blowing his eagle whistle
beckoning to the ancestors from
the four directions
the four directions in between

a two-spirit sundance leader
at an all-women's sundance
enters the arbor at sunup
through the east gate
the story of a lifetime
a picture window
out from behind the wind

as long as this sleigh ride

certain stories
whose power resides inside
every telling, every teller
shift the sound of crickets
the breath around a drum

they're breeding themselves
into extinction, the elder said
just before pointing out that place
where the owl comes
to bring the spirits home

so many babies are born
that way, with a fear of their own
whiteness, along the edges of
the milky way, surrounded by
the northern lights
at dawn

we have too much to do
to continue to be dragged down
by old home feelings creeping
seeping through our day-to-day
all them causes and effects

at one time scientists thought
whoever had the largest brain
was the smartest
till their experiments revealed
who had the largest brains
was the inuit and the whales

all them this's
and therefore the that's
a long, slow, unencumbered view
of the past, the fine, delicate touches
from fingertips that heal, the voices
of the ancestors

resounding around us
the us's and the them's
leading the way into a future
filled with four-directions youth
red black yellow white, who know
the only words that count
are those ones spoken
from the heart

spiders

the spider's web is a physical construct which many native cultures
draw on symbolically to imbed this principle in their storytelling as an
expression of the creative process concerned with the connectedness
of all things.

jeannette armstrong and douglas cardinal

first thing this morning
a brown striped spider
crossed my path
between my bedroom and the bath

I picked her up, thanked her
her afraid of my dry, salt-palm
I put her outside
her body the shape of métis
infinity
her eight legs
the four directions of the wind
the medicine wheel

not ten minutes earlier
between waking and asleep
I dreamed I was inside my house
inside my heart and body
where spirit resides
where each season
each rock and tree and leaf
listens to the sound that life makes
within these walls

I dreamed my house fell
face first
onto the ground
baby spiders all around

I was reminded of last summer
a large black spider, weighted down
by her babies on her back
so many tiny eyes looking up
into mine

they seemed to be talking
all talking at once, their voices
a quiet drone, a storyteller's tone
the storyteller's role is to draw a story
out of the listener, they said
all in unison

I kept blinking my eyes against the sun
sweat pooling inside my ears
and I heard them again
they said, a great deal of a story
is there, you see, inside the listener

two young two-spirit girls walked up just then
their eyes wide, their joy like a tune
their laughter, loud and long
filling the spaces, pushing their voices down
through their bellies and feet through the ground

they'd written a play
those two young two-spirit girls
they performed that play for the spiders there
their little black bodies moving in time
to the movements of the two-spirit girls

who joined together
in an eight-legged dance
weaving the future

a spider's web, heart-shaped
life's strength, all nations
all races, all genders
all ours, they said

the two young two-spirit girls
their voices beat, beat beating
we got the rhythm of the planet, us
we got the road to peace
hey-ya-hey-ya-hey-eh-hey-ya-hey-ya-hey
hey-ya-hey-ya-hey-eh-hey-ya-hey-ya-hey
hey-ya-hey-ya-hey
hey-ya-hey-ya-hey-ya-hey-hey-hey-yo

spiders 2

at a 1995 international meeting of elders, rose auger demonstrated the power of feminine spirituality. during the council one of her spider guardians, who always accompanies her to listen and help, hopped onto the lap of a young holy man, who began to tremble. as he reached out to swat the spider – an unthinkably brutal act – an elder sitting next to him gently picked the creature up and handed it back to rose. she smiled and prophesied that during the final days of earth's forthcoming purification, spider will return to correct what has gone wrong with the younger generation.

babara tedlock

it started again at my first fast
I was cooking there, me, not fasting
spiraling up that mountain
in first gear, too steep for second
stopping along the way
to cool off the engine
overcast at full moon, so
no light, just the head lights
hey, might as well be usin freakin
pin lights, says my cuz, for all the good these brights
light up the rock up here
it's like drivin blind, vertical like
like we're gonna fall down behind us, lost
laughing at me, he says whatever you do, don't look down
I know you, cuz
you'll never come back down this mountain
if you do
so I keep my eyes on the windshield of the car
the road, on the sheer rock wall beside me
her curves, straight up, the certainty of
protection, of prayer, commitment

on the top of that mountain next morning
sun's yellow air on every side
inside me, an old people's path
spiraling around, down that same mountain
lighting up the stone, then a yellow spider
so full of the medicine there
throwing out a thin silver line, caught by the wind
to float great distances
landing far below, beyond the valley's song

before I see her, I feel the elder arrive
feel her broad red hat, her turquoise, her black boots
her power
I know things about her I do not understand
like her soul is an ancient tree
her bones an eye for the spirits
after two days, she calls for me to come see her
in her trailer, and all I can do is wonder how
she hauled that trailer up that mountain

she tells me, she says my name is rose auger
I'm a cree from driftpile, every morning
I'm hearing less and less people want to sleep
in your tipi, they're afraid
on account of the spiders, eh
you put together offerings, you
my sister, she'll show you how
I want to talk to you

when I see her in her trailer the following day
tea, buns, bologna, she says, I hear you're surrounded
by spiders every sunrise
anyone peaceful, and you are peaceful, my girl
has a troubled past, but that's not why we're here
it's not how long you live, but how you live your life
until you pass, but you already know these things

out the window of her trailer I can see
moisture rising up the valley, the greens there
the yellows, rich still, despite the late fall heat
how to be kind against all the odds, she says
now tell me, you, tell me about you and spiders
you are surrounded by spiders every morning
I'm hearing they form a circle
on the canvas of the tipi, above your head
is this true

I tell her, yes, after my mom passed
my kids and I moved into a little house
so many spiders on the outside there
the greens of the siding woven with
delicate words I'd never seen
that's when it all starts, when spider
makes her way up and into me
his yellows a knowing, reminding me
of my womanhood, my responsibilities
to the mysteries, the ancestors
those who came before and those to follow
on the other side

she says, yes, my girl, you've got a lot yet to say
continue to pray, call on the grandmothers there
stay on that good red road
not easy, that, but hey, you came from hell and back
you'll write your way to wisdom, you
you'll be asked to help the women
the children, find their way
and remember, spider holds the women's medicine
power, knowledge that you'll need, so pray
welcome spider into your world every day
as you age, you'll know more of
why I spoke to you today

hers was a smile of morning

so the road which determines our value
is usually the one with the briar patch,
the hard road proving to ourselves we have
what it takes to be a success.
rita joe

this your story, she asks, rita joe does, reaching
deep into her blue, blue housecoat pocket, puts a book
my first book, next to her bacon and eggs
poking her index finger there, then up at me
sit, you, she says, I want to talk to you

this is the day after her final book launch
says she's ready to retire, too tiring this
with her parkinson's now
too much travel, and wasn't that great
there when that pigeon comes in out
of this october cold, right on through that window
up there, struts into that faculty club, pooping
all over the round of the blue of the floor
all them three piece suits runnin
like hell for the door

pokes my first book with her index finger
you look at me with your eyes, there, you
I've got something to say to you, you
have a goodness about you, deep inside
that goodness can't be touched, or hurt
or cast aside, you're surrounded by a clear
blue light, bright like the moon
some spiritual leaders, there, don't like this
them, one look your way, their own flaws
popping out at them like pimples
on a newborn baby's smooth, brown butt

this is the day after my neighbour next door
proud to be from newfoundland
runs outside in her stocking feet
my boy leading rita joe by the arm
over ice and snow, neighbour blocks their way
to say, who's your guest, here
leans over rita joe, eye to eye
you look like you got a bit a indian in ya

she says to me, rita joe that day
she's involved with her son at home, there
in the sacred ways of her people
and she wants me to know here today
when you're asked to make that kind of sacrifice
I was asked to make as a child
you're rewarded ten-fold
pokes my first book with her index finger
you keep writing, my girl, you catch those words
that float their way through the air to you

this is the day after she says, rita joe
to that neighbour of mine from newfoundland
I'm one hundred per cent mi'kmaq indian
my boy says, and she's famous, too
order of canada, met the queen, awards
degrees piled up to the sky, wait
says that neighbour of mine from newfoundland
I wanna get me camera, get a shot of ya
next to me, out over there
by my own front door

she moves her hands, rita joe that day
onto each side of my face, her index fingers
pressing next to my ears, I can still feel
them there to this day, you listen, you
I'll expect to see many more books from you
you promise me this, my girl
creator has given you the gift for words
you share, there, you follow that road
past the briar patch, out into the blue
blue sky of this new october day

october day, rita joe's last poem, found
on her typewriter after she passed
on the day I am blue,
I go again to the wood where the tree is swaying,
arms touching you like a friend,
and the sound of the wind so alone like I am;
whispers here, whispers there,
come and just be my friend.

piitakii ikwa moniyaw: a triptych

what happens in the future affects what happens in the present.
daniel david moses

1.

I once dreamed I was an eagle in flight
a futuristic dream
learned how to be still
in the middle of a prairie sand storm
smack in the heart of the bible belt

the game they call democracy
can't go there where there's
meaning past the lines
across the page
past the in between
their monologue
deep as soup powder
in a dried up pond

the rich have stolen
even the mirage
off the heat on the highway
even the guilt

to speak the words
tell the world, write up the names
a national registry
open those lines all muddled
coated and knotted
like hair half way down the back
tangled and tied and confused
from being so long without love

2.

I once dreamed I was an eagle
a futuristic dream
my head and shoulders eagle
my own body sitting on a rock
I created a facial tattoo
coveted by the white man
yet grotesque enough
to frighten any child, anyone

a tattoo whose ink
so putrid, so decayed, so decomposed
the seers would say
even the fundamental shift
in space and time
even mother earth
would know the power of this ink

to make the white man pay with land
those debts they owe
to make them do, not physical labour
but grueling healing work
to earn alterations to the stench
or rot their faces
from the eyelids down

3.

I once dreamed I was an eagle
clinging to a west coast red cedar
with weendigo, a permanent scream
a futuristic dream
flew right into ottawa me and that tree
weendigo and that scream
saw fish without fins, fish without dreams
frozen inside river ice
behind parliament hill

the farmers and townfolk and suburbs
along the way, creeping ever forward
draining swamps ahead of them
capping artesian wells
weendigo and that scream
posting signs
as long as white people work the land
every day they destroy
by their hand

why do white people
say, I'm sorry
build their cities and freeways
where the waters gather
starve lakes, damn rivers, cannon hail

why do white people
say, I'm sorry
seep ahead of themselves
as coastal buildings leak into the sea

gone with the weendigo
gone with a scream

e s a r i n t u l o m d p c f b
v h g j q z y x k w

hand in hand
the letters cross the room
whirl around the bed
sweep past the window
wriggle across the wall
swoop to the door
and return to begin again

jean-dominique bauby *

I am so happy I could die
is what she said just before the round hole
in the ground exploded with bees
this is how I hear the world
tiny commas squirming to poke their way
through the whites of the eyes of the page
letters leaping off a chalk board

in thin white streams, like headphones
dangling from the ears of self-conscious youth
texting parents and friends under
500-count sheets, grasping only the sounds
of the light from a daytime moon
even from there, e=mc2
where energy equals mass times

the velocity of light squared
who cares
the numbers just don't add up, you see
higher mathematics, the queen's english
eating at the holes
around babies' empty bellies
middle class starvation of millions

the latest in honey-sweet jeans
why not blame it on government thieves
or adopt an african child, dry snow
building a mountain of toys
jetsetters helping kids to be kids
this is kanata, eh
where bees are just fancy dancers

who see out from 5 different eyes
their ultraviolet views and colour hues
the music of letters their prize
while an old indian woman
hears bees' song, says
if people around the world
were to take the time
to pray for the healing of earth

8 hours is all we would need
8 hours of prayer
8 hours without greed
to feed those millions of people
heal the core of our mother the earth

locked-in by the wasting of time
we return to begin again
swoop to the door
wriggle across the wall
sweep past the window
whirl around the bed
the letters cross the room
hand in hand

z x j q k v b p g y w f m c u l
d r h s o n i a t e

* after suffering a massive stroke at age 43 in 1995, jean-
dominique bauby, editor of french elle magazine, became
paralyzed from head to toe, and was diagnosed with "locked-
in syndrome." the only part of his body he could move was
his left eye, from side to side, and to blink. bauby wrote his
memoir, *the diving bell and the butterfly*, by blinking at the
letter he wanted while claude mendibil, a freelance book
editor, spoke the alphabet, one letter at a time. the letters at
the beginning of the poem are those as they appear in order
of frequency of use in french (as she recited them to him) and
at the end of the poem, the letters are in order of frequency in
english – but listed backwards.

it was set before her birth

once upon a time
there was balance
then there was evolution
and balance became
frozen in T.I.M.E.

shirley bear

it is true that talking changes everything
the old people tell us that language is sacred
what you write, what you say, even what you think
so be careful, they say, know that what goes out
into the air, onto the page, cannot be taken back
cannot be rearranged or erased or burned
in a fire

I am a sundancer, something I've never said out loud
to a crowd or in a public way, in a story
in the shape of a poem, until now
when I'm almost sixty
before I dance
I help for several years
help the women dancers, content to serve
the servants

one evening
I go to my tent
cover my face with my sleeping bag, try to sleep
can't, look out the screen at grandma moon
full and swollen
everything, the grasses, the trees, glowing
like water on the ground

there's smoke making its own path
moving with such tenderness, as if alive
right up and into my tent, and I think
maybe I'm meant to visit the fire
so I go there, where people are sleeping
I offer tobacco to that sacred fire, look over
at the centre tree

see each touch of my foot on the earth, a sacred touch
of death, and therefore life
reminding me of a dream, my dream from years ago
of me, sundancing, my hair long and silver
down my back, the times
year after year, praying while the dancers dance
ancient women behind me, to the west, their voices
their power, unveiling the distance
to the other side

like the old basket where my grandmother
kept her ribbons, her wool, her embroidery threads
her hands, stitching stories into cloth, that old basket
has memories too, she would say, songs
and I could hear them, those songs
as if behind our lives, others live theirs
the mysteries

they tell us, do not be afraid, the old ones do, as the worlds
will blur and you may witness amazing things
pray, they say, pray and remember why you are alive
to feel the limits of your existence in this life, and remember
ceremony brings permanent, positive change in a person's life
whether that person acknowledges it
or not

only good white people need apply

calgary herald, august 2010
the plane rocking like a train
as I read those words

I like to think that we're all pretty

"only good white people need apply"
over the shoulder of the white man
in a three piece suit

much the same

as when I get home I have a dream
I'm in the centre
of a medicine wheel

colour is a good thing

says the elder
from the heart of something
like stonehenge

just look around

there are people in a circle
my ancestors
from here and overseas

wouldn't it be a drag if we saw

from the inside out
like everyone has their own sun
the people all lit up

only in black & white

> I crack a joke
> laughter all around
> white teeth on brown

only one skin color

> I can still hear the discord of those
> calgary herald words in my head
> like wasps eating wings off butterflies

like eating cornflakes every day

> moonless night light humming grief
> good white people's ears closed to that sound
> mitigwakik daywaygun whispers on

jillian good eagle

forty thousand feet

when I was an undergrad, I learned
there are certain things you don't talk about
in a poem, like native peoples, child sexual abuse
womanly things, like childbirth or menopause
depression or rape, dismal things that alienate
your audience

tonight, westjest flight 655
montréal to calgary, couldn't have known
this unbearable delight
flying from darkness into the light
an orange horizon, bending
beneath a crescent so blue, so bright
mother earth's belly, full and black
the simple joy of nighttime
kept at bay, that opening there
a northern star suspended

time changed inside that star
from the window seat of the westjet plane
I saw
things from my own past, my ancestors'
my infancy, years of terror inside rain

*i'm five. when i'm thinking i'm someone special they
put me in the chicken coop. i make up that name myself:
chicken coop. i think it's funny. i like chickens. i try to stay
happy in the chicken coop. can't stand up. can't lie down.
i squat. I'm a chicken. i feel funny too. i laugh too and
my arms love to flap around. i'm a chicken in the chicken
coop. when i come out from the foggy in my head i see
the other kid. big big hurting. the kid is above me. i see
my own face above the barbed wire. can't touch the other
kid. I am the other kid. can't reach her. can't help her.
can't help. it's my fault. they tell me it's my fault.*

i won't do what i'm told. my beating heart breathe small
my beating heart breathe small hate hate i hate me. I hate
me. i hate it. i hate it.
kill it.

a walking path, between awake and asleep
I slipped into that star, with ease
three, four hours on that westjet plane
there were priests in there
from another time
priests there of all kinds
corralling the one-and-a-half men
the one-and-half women, children, the babes

they'd say, here we are, us, straining our star-voices
to be heard, us otepayemsuak, us métis
those are half-indian, half-white, half-devil
those priests would say, pray
because them, they couldn't do
a darn thing with us otepayemsuak, us métis
except beat us, rape us, make us pay for their sins

hard to believe, but easier to swallow
with bottled water, pretzels, cookies
hard liquor, six bucks a shot
at forty thousand feet
then publishers, voyeurs, explorers of forget-me-nots
get wind of our métis stories
want details, but not too much
can this really be true
want the sensation of it all, but
not too much, have to tone the story down

publisher: your sample – I'm going by memory at the moment as I don't have your piece before me – you talk about ritual abuse and abuse at the hands of the canadian military. now a piece that discusses abuse by the military (mental, physical, forced drug experimentation and the like), we could accept as these are issues with a lot broader evidence to support the claims.

inside that star, there were judges, too
the ones from ontario criminal injuries
compensation board, back in '98, nice people
came, talked to me of crime and torture and flashback
ritualized abuse, the military's psychiatrists
cold war mind control, torture of little children
experiments they called, "project bluebird"
tweet-tweet, terror, torture
there isn't a day goes by
that I don't think
their meagre monetary award
will never give me back
my life

us, we're over saskatchewan now
forty thousand feet
that star still inside my pain
medical records peeking out from
years inside a file, forget-them-not
says the buffalo, the old priests
praying for the glory of god

editorial team for side effects: *we read your draft. what we felt was missing was an example or two of the ritual abuse you suffered, some content of your flashbacks. you need not be overly graphic, but this would give some grounding to your discussion of flashbacks.*

another paper turned down, too lifelike, too
too true, keep trying, the grandmothers tell me
put it all down in a poem
us otepayemsuak, us métis, we do
what's right us, despite the fight
me, I write, that's what I do, a nokomis too
there in photos and right up close, I look pretty
ordinary, fearless, I like the colour red
piano solo playing in my ear
me, my sense of humour, my rich spiritual ties
that star is reaching, teaching of brighter days

i'm seven. i hate me. how long did it take? seven years.
seven years of bad luck. i stare at myself in that mirror.
smash that mirror with my fists. hate. i hate me. hate. hate.
hate. i hate you i hate you i hate you. kill it. cut cut cut it
up. i want to die. i want to die.
kill it.

travels skyward, that first northern star
same one out there from this westjet plane
mirror mirror on the wall
torture through my early years
pushing babies' pain, children's pain
tough guys, them army shrinks
safe inside their doctor's garb, barbed wire

people don't want to believe
canada's trusted
priests, whose oaths, all heavenly, glorious hosts
doctors, whose professional, ethical oaths
tortured my ancestors
tortured me

this is my poetry, my lifestory, my medical file

from medical file: this patient suffers from post traumatic
stress disorder. she is a survivor of severe childhood abuse,
which includes:
1. sophisticated torture over a period of nine years,
including having her hands and/or feet squeezed in a vice-
like device causing unbearable pain.
2. put in a cage where she was unable to sit or lie (only
squat) for up to two days.
3. hung by her wrists for up to three days.
4. confined in a small, cold space and left without food or
water for up to three days.
5. placed in a large room with high ceilings and narrow
horizontal windows at the top of the walls for days at a
time, woken at all hours of the day and night, fed at all
hours of the day and night and exposed to loud noises and
music at irregular intervals.
6. received severe, repeated beatings.
7. sexually assaulted by multiple adult perpetrators from
infancy until the age of eleven.
8. exposed to long-term isolation.
9. lowered into coffins with decomposing bodies.
10. lowered into outhouses, where she was left for long
periods of time.

I am a poet, working
to make change, to speak out

our spirits helping us
know what we must do

I ask, how do we make something beautiful
from so much pain

a world of red

a gifted cree warrior woman once told me
when she was a child

her eyes were bleeding onto the pages
of an atlas at school, rearranging rivers

pushing lakes through to the pages below
the pages before that looking back

to the yellow of the world, turning red
on teacher's precious book

columbus's "new world"
the blood of the taino people, eight million

to twenty-eight thousand
in twenty years, the bones of millions

of native slaves, warriors, children, babes
of millions of millions of hundreds of millions

their red drops on the maps of the white man
soaked through to a future

where resistance moves beyond the road
beyond the talk, beyond the milky way

NIA:WEN-NYAWA, MEEGWICH MES ƟTEPAYEMSUAK

old bones in the poop deck

the cree called the métis apeytogosan, which means 'half-people.'
the cree also coined another term for the métis – otepayemsuak
– meaning the 'independent ones' or as the métis themselves put
it – 'the bosses of themselves.' to the cree, the métis were known
as otepayemsuak because their communities were distinct from
both the non-indian and indian communities.
jean teillet

cont.

since 1500 and 64
my grandmothers
indian, breed, métisse
are some 400 and 14

germaine proulx
 rosina lafrance
  anna lafrance
   elizabeth trottier
    adelaide durocher
     catherine brazeau
      josephte larocque
       jeanne pilon
        marie gaillard
         nom de l'espousé inconnu
          jacqueline pajot
           charlotte gauthier
            exilda dufort
             barbe duchesne
              guillemette raynier
               marie pinel de la chaunaie

in 1600 and 22
2 claudes
after 50 and 8 years
return from geneve suisse
to live among the iroquois
2 claudes are grandchildren
of the people
their grandmothers
captured by the french

in 1600 and 44
2 claudes
are welcomed as a couple
as lovers are
they have a child
whose name is barbe

barbe duchesne
marie badel
charlotte pilon
charlotte barbe seguin
pelagie tougas dit laviolette
nom de l'espousé inconnu
jeanne agnier
marie anne tabeau
genevieve cadieu
marguerite brigitte groulx
josephte lalonde
marie-josephe ranger dit laplante
marie malepart
esther leduc
exilda dufort

in 1800 and 44
7 generations later
exilda is born

exilda's daughter is rosina lafrance
rosina's mother-in-law is
rosina's cousin
rosina's greatgrandparents are
rosina's mother-in-law's parents
rosina's mother-in-law is
anna lafrance

in 1900 and zero 3
3 years after the fire comes
across the bridge
and into ottawa from hull
rosina has 2 daughters
18 years apart
germaine the older girl
3 months after her parents
are married in the rectory
of the church à l'ottawa

germaine proulx
marie-anne dubois
nom de l'espousé inconnu

                    catherine plante
                  angelique leroy
                 cecile groulx
               anne julienne dumont
                marie morin
               anne goguet
              marie riton
                louise garnier
               esther leduc
                  marie-josephe laviolette
                terese dube
                   petronille senecal
                  pelagie laviolette

in 1900 and 40
germaine the older girl
is gifted
is two-spirit
her 6 children
2 of whom are twins
scooped from their mom
their dad their grandparents
sisters brothers cousins
auntys uncles friends
lives with her companion
martha from downtown
some 40 years
they call themselves
mmes sauvageaux
which is a joke

                  anne guillaume
                 jeanne charron
                 anne girardin
                marie brazeau
                marie gauthier
                 charlotte barbe seguin
                marie langlois
               jeanne lepine
              renee loppee
             barbe beauvais
            marie brazeau

nom de l'espousé inconnu
marie de la chaunaie
marie pomponnelle
marie blanchard
jeanne lepine

in 1900 and 40 too
germaine the older girl
whose 6 children
2 of whom are twins
are scooped and fostered out
the government people say
strangers must raise up these kids
as farmslaves
for english-speaking irish whites

catherine de laporte
jeanne sasquestee
angelique leroy
francoise hebert
marie brisebois
cecile groulx
suzanne miguad
anne julienne dumont
genevieve cadieux
petronille senecal
marie proulx
marie morin
sara cousseau
nom de l'espouse inconnu
louise esnard
francoise boucher

since 1900 and 40 too
les personnes des grands-parents
ne sont pas connus
of germaine the older girl
whose grandmothers
2 claudes
return from geneve suisse
to live among the iroquois

even mosquitoes sleep at night

two snowy owls fly tight together
land there, on the heat of the runway
their voices the red of the sky
embellishing their thoughts
through story

mosquitoes live in the greens
say those snowy owls
they eat there: fruit nectars
plant sugars, the blood
the ladies use for their babes

not like the olden times, there
when mosquito was a giant
ate humans then, snowy owls too
some humans say a woman burned
that giant, and maybe she did

but us, too, we burned her
that was before her ashes turned on us
each with her own tiny hum
a penetrating song, her harmony
a bitter, biting, bingo

which is why we'll hunt
in the heat of a summer day
why we like airports and rooftops
where mosquitoes stay at bay
keeps us young
keeps our winter whites
from going gray
I laugh and I wonder, me
is this how I'll age
backwards and into a youthful

old lady of childhood glee
winter to fall to summer to
memories of my children's
my grandchildren's childhoods
so much healthier than my own

the yellow eyes of snowy owl, years and years
of setting suns, my childhood homeland
mosquitoes big as the ottawa
odauwau zeepih, ktchisipi
her waters wide as a lake

mosquitoes big as the petawawa
abeed waewae zeepih
her coming sound
accentuating my vision, night and day
those little flies, bending the seasons

don't go too far from their watery nests, them
follow me indoors as I write
my own blood biting me in clusters
around the words that utter themselves
from the depths of my own water
still standing

they say I'm just a teacher

i) fireflies at full moon

"my friend and myself are one," the mohawk says. "there are not two of us; we are one heart encircled by the warm, light-giving rays of the sun."
e. pauline johnson

the teachings of sundance
year after year
a thousand caresses
whose timeless hold
pushes pebbles up from the red, hot centre
of the mother
along that line where land and water entwine
their love a knowing
a chickadee in flight

this morning at sunrise I heard someone imitating a chickadee.
the voice was softer, higher-pitched, more musical. right away I
knew it was an imitator and I thought, wow, that kid is good.
so I went to the window and what did I see? a magpie staring
back at me. and as if to be sure we were sure she was she, that
magpie sang again in chickadee for me.

just then I could clearly see
our métis ancestors
inside those sounds
the light from their bodies
illuminating a road
to certainty

back then, you called me your soul mate. and although I was
uncertain what that might mean, it was like our friendship had
been there – thousands of years – waiting for us to meet. the
sacred fire. the sacred lodge. the sacred pipe. the solitude. the
ancestors.

two middle-aged two-spirit métis women who were called
in our youth to this way of life. who love the rocks, the
wood, the fire, the water. the pit, the mound, the lodge. the
humour. the work, the prayers. the honour and privilege.
the sacrifice.

did you know the root of the word métis
is greek
but I'm nobody's fool
they say I'm just a teacher
the way the morning sky
embraces the deep, dark arch of a chinook
on the hottest day of the year
her yellow-eyed horizon
beckoning a late-day sun
our friendship reflected there

and there, too, I could clearly see
a cup of strong, hot tea
and adam lambert on the tube
ancestors inside the haze
the light from their bodies
fireflies at full moon
in the long, wet grass

ii) there were more songs in my mouth

since time began, the mohawks have always likened friendship to the sun. sun is exalted in the heavens, the power of heat, of light, of strength. without the sun, this world would not continue to exist.
e. pauline johnson

there were more songs in my mouth
after centuries of sleeping
in a much deeper earth
eyes to the wind
where the edges of time
loosened around a red
red sunrise
whose shadows on the trees
on the walls
under the bed

woke me from sleep. I'd had a dream where I was at
sundance – a woman's sundance where all the women were
wearing green – all the dancers – and at the same time
all the dancers were trees. I was overcome by a feeling of
deep gratitude to the women, to the trees, for offering their
prayers and for making such a sacrifice.

and out you walked from the skin of the rain
what you look at is what you become
you said
and to speak out an animal's name
is to call out
the medicines, the powers inside

then you reached out to me
in a watery way
and you began to say
I think I love you, my friend
tell me this one thing
here in the heat of the day
tell me, why do you sundance

I woke from the dream at the touch of your hand, though
I can tell you now that I sundance because I know when
I'm there that our prayers are heard by the ancestors –
by those who help us survive the losses, the devastation.
because I know mother earth hears our sacred songs,
feels our healing medicines through the soles of our feet,
spreading out and into her belly, into the air. because I'm
certain I'm doing the right thing when I'm there.
one heart. one drum. the heartbeat of mother earth.
because I am one moment on this earth when there is life
beyond the seen and a love that knows no bounds.

and so, my friend, I speak to you now
in this full light of the sun
where nothing is hidden
or held back
where dreams are for people
what water is for trees

where the medicine waits
to greet our skin's longing
at the meeting of the years
on the threshold
of our aging

iii) like prayer cloths

without friendship, the mohawk holds that the heart of a person
would be the bleached, colourless, bloodless thing that a plant is
when grown in the dark.

e. pauline johnson

love is a prickly road, mother water will say, and every spring,
thistles find their way into the darkness of the lodge, their
stems dulled and white, their growth stunted and twisted,
hugging the moisture along the ground – the breath of the
ancestors having fallen there, filling out their harmonies,
calling out their songs.

outside the lodge
thistles thrive
their roots are nutritious
their flower buds, delicious
sweetgrass and sage both love to grow
in the sweet, soft soil
the thistle makes

next to old cottonwoods
who suckle like babies
on the mother water
under the ground

the mother water
whose long, limber lines
make their way
up through the dark bark
like prayer cloths
promises of a sunrise
reflected in the intricate veins
of each winded leaf

reminding me that I've sundanced in wind like that, and
though people told me later they thought surely I'd blow away,

I felt rooted to the ground like a cottonwood, my eagle feather fan singing sacred songs throughout my body, my pores open to the past, to the future.

but that was here, on the plains
not up camel's hump mountain
where red maple graces us
greets us in our dreams
our spirits mingle in the night
where monarchs, up before the dawn
fold their orange wings
around the sun
a simple gesture
of friendship

and there we sit before ceremony, beneath the old centre tree, her maple touching the arbor, enveloping the younger tree with eyes that see beyond you and me, her red words reaching deep into the mother. like the red maple, us métis, we grow to suit the land. where we are, we make the land our home, our roots dug deep into the heart of the mother water. we tell her of friendships, of the comings and goings of women and love. love is a stony road, mother water will say, as she touches the footprints left here by two old friends, whose roots enfold, hold years of teachings, blood and bone.

iv) snakes waving their one-footed bodies

stronger than her hate, stronger than her revenge, stronger than
her love, stronger than death itself, is the friendship of a red
indian.

e. pauline johnson

just before my first time at women's sundance, I had a
dream where I'd place my hand on the surface of a table
and I'd leave the wet paw print of a wolf. I drove there,
alone – from alberta to vermont. along the way I learned
the trees who hug the highway are called a vanity belt.

driving on the wrong side
of corn
where mystery is a form
of power
the milky way's shadow
of a life
that's bound by sleep and dreams

on the road I dreamed a snowy owl in flight, her wings
reaching around my thoughts, my grandmothers' voices
travelling from the stars, transforming thought to word to
song.

like the owl
my sight in the night
is better than in
the light of day

we, you and me, met in the dark
at full moon
wrapped inside air
like sap inside a leaf
held there

drinking from the stray
spray of life
heat building along the edges
of the trees

that night I dreamed I was holding a buffalo skull and I
could feel the life of the bull through the bone. the skull
was mine, a gift given to me and kept in a place of honour.
I woke to a spray of purple grasses, their light reflected
against deep, heavy storm clouds bursting with fire and
rain, the thunderbeings ready, reaching out into our hearts
with ancient teachings of touch and tenderness.

that day you were made
my mentor
a teacher in this life
whose buffalo medicine
the essence of friendship
goes head first into a storm

today, our friendship deepens, electric movement in our
feet. the climb up the hill, walking with us still, as we
write our way – a sudden downpour. snakes waving their
one-footed bodies in harmony with the mother. life is full
of surprises. life is full of gifts.

we are our own life stories
here to entertain
here to instruct
here to heal
ours a rhythm in the night

for bonnie fabian

looking down through the window of a plane

I have a dream where I wake up laughing
then I dream I'm able to walk on top of great lake waters
open my eyes to the stillness of snow lingering
around the trunks of trees and inside rocks, so far below
grandmother moon full still, her silver light swelling with the wind
her circular songs rewriting the sky whose morning red pours out
through her throat in water words, their lines unwinding
for each person's life is as sacred as a woman
who sits at the foot of a tree, peering down through to that sky

childhood longings, broad strokes of red painted onto black
scratches reveal a world of colour and light
whole melodies pushed under the bed, waiting there for wind
blowing, calling, calling out a story of what it is
to be born between the worlds, a tree inside my eyes
whose sky folds its blues around my red, red heart

looking down through the plane window, I hear the keys of a piano
fingers whose tips are the ears of air, then small scribbles of snow
the sun's reflection, like a syllabic language written on the ground
defying the gridlines imposed on the round palm of the land
where the wind on the ice sends messages skyward

more water, more ice, words refracted for the birds to read
for the star people, and, in the spring light, the snow around the trees
accentuates their greens and, oh, the ottawa, and as the plane descends
I know, us métis, we always like to live by the water
in my bones, I know why, not just for transportation
but for life

take exit 82

overdressed and happy
I feel the thunderbeings
hear their song
touch their prayer
my lips holding the air
my movements slow, cautious
electricity that dreams

when the curbs are indistinguishable
from the roads
the stone opens to reveal the moon
a lover's arch filled with the hum of bees
even sky has a kind of water
falling through its bone hands
that have nothing to hold onto

I hear a crow outside the car window
hear how the underground rivers run
from seed to green, cocoon to flight
a view from above, the air wet and thin
along the offramps, along the horizon
too bright to look at while waiting to fill with rain

the wet roads
life seeping through to the floor of the sea
where a young diver tries to break a record
for underwater depth
while millions starve, without clean water to drink
around the billboards and buses and big screen tv's

I sit and in my heart
feel the hum of the engine
the métis grandmothers around me
who love the water, the land
who love language and song
how they teach us the healing plants
how sometime they will show us
how to renew the shattered world

you can see that lake in the sky

margaret atwood is looking
a lot like the queen these days
dragging the furniture of plot
from room to room

writing is everywhere, I once heard her say
on the side of a box in the grocery store
at the side of the road on a sign
underfoot on the sidewalks
on walls and ceilings, on buildings too
flying through the sky on a plane

I had a teacher once, aritha van herk
who introduced me to margaret atwood
her poetry, not her prose
there and then I knew, we need poetry
to speak out our spirits, help us know
what we must do

aritha van herk, young and fresh
and tough, an icon now
views the world
out of different coloured eyes
this is no essay, she said
in her teacherly, red script
but you sure as hell can write

me learning disabled, dyslexic too
can't spell worth beans
couldn't have known
those small, red words
would water the rest of my life
like an open great lake
steam rising skyward
couldn't have known
I'd be the clouds that drink
that great lake's water

only to fall again as summer rain
onto the v of a tree
nests showing through the growing greens
their couplets not rhyming by happenstance
with a thunderbird nest at sundance

mazie horsefall meets fred wah

sentenced to light
breathin my name with a sigh
is a door
fred wah

I took three poetry writing classes with fred wah
a canadian idol so renowned I saw his name on a big sign
it was pouring rain, dark night, these bright, bright
lights at the side of the road, flashing his name
his fame up the whole highway, down onto the wet roads
of crowchild trail, the armed forces museum
flashing red, fred, his name reflecting onto a fighter plane
tilted towards the sky, its wing a wah

this is a good twenty years before my baby granddaughter
says to her mom, she says, mom, I want to go to a moo-seum
her mom says, mazie, what's a moo-seum
and she says, where the cows live, silly

make it strange, he'd say, fred wah
explore the dialogical, propioception
all yellow on the black chalk board
lead to new poetics, new concepts, drama
heroes, perhaps, whose many voices going on
and on and on and on
at the same time, projective verse, he'd say
do not be afraid to create something new

so mazie says to her mom, she says, so r u
having another baby, and her mom says, no
but your tummy is big, mommy, so her mom says
hey, I'm just fat, don't rub it in
that mazie laughs and laughs, says
I'm gonna rub it innnnn, starts rubbing
the air in a circle, haw, haw, haw, mom, I'm rubbin it in

reader becomes agent of apprehending meaning
says fred, and apprehension is anxiety, art
coming into the abstract, the artist gives
the audience power, hints, slow language at work
not to be afraid to show the framework

mazie's in the closet
furiously looking for something
raises her hands to her head, shakes them
cheese and whiskers, she says
whaddam I a gonna do

do not be afraid to expose yourself inside the line
mixing, mixing, mewing media, the journalist
sliding into a kind of poetry, a personal reportage
like meditation, fred wah, he showed us
don't tell those words, don't yell the old lyric line
from the snowy tops of the rockies
white pages blown across the plains
more something nitty, gritty

puts a colouring sheet of snow white
in front of her face, mazie does
starts talking to her infant
brother as snow white
goes over to her mom, says
hey, I'm snow white, paint me, mom

the seeds of maize and beans

an early morning dream
gathering her long hair
into one hand

deep cold lingers
old words that carry
rich, wet sand
ocean floor's floating
out moon's crescent
the road of life

two clouds
their thin lines
the only light in the sky

flying into the dawn
unbound by ink or page
a hum, a scent
seeing out many eyes
wings that carry teeth
listening for silence
deep with blue sun

wait for birth with an open mind

there are more than a few people who feel strengthened and consoled
by having their sense of reality affirmed and transfigured by art.
susan sontag

I was born on a dining room table, formal-like
into the smells of roast duck, green beans, onions, apple pie
not my parents' linoleum table overtop the vinyl floor
next to the ironing board
but at the doctor's house, my small mouth crying
lines from a poem
a hole through the floor from a cane

the hole perfectly round
how fast intelligence travels
right from the start I needed help talking
every inside line moving at a pace that pulls
at the skin, eats through smiles and eyes that die
with every blink

try to hide the shame
almost silent, almost watery green
open like a lightening bolt
that's burned its way across the sky
out from my eyes, wide open
facing down, like thought woman

mon dieu, c'est grotesque, I heard her say
my face still encased, attached to the sac
drinking the light there, a reflection of the blue
pulling something new into my mouth, my tongue, my lungs
and my mother's cry from the table top
no one will come near her like this
an evil full of lightning, full of song

but that was then, the table's deep mahogany
always thinking, always green
where spring waits for trees
like some blossoms burst the air with bees
a mother's hate that goes beyond mere fear

and even today, even all these years later
if I can feel so alive, how can I not know where
shame's smallest exits beg to be placed
crowded together, their paper words' unaired questions
covered over with ink

there's a reason everyone dies at birth

deep inside her there was nowhere to hide
exposed by an opening in the trees
a change of inner weather, cold air
barely touching her, from calves to heart
and back again
the quiet before prairie rain

I want it all, she said out loud
the richness that startles small black beetles
pushing their bodies across the water
toward the shore
only to be caught up by tadpoles
seeking limbs

there, on the surface of the water
the moon was smaller than the clouds
and she thought she might vanish
from her body's hiding place

maybe it was spider who helped her
pulled her out from the corner of her room
took away those four walls
piled now like stones across her path

there was evil in this world
in the shape of humans
but she was no longer afraid of her past
her future, reluctant to let go
of her mother

her ache so great she wanted to
hurt it, hurt herself
where sometimes she felt tender, old
where sometimes they shared laughter
in the darkness, faces lit up by the moon

she looked out on the water as if the answers
were there, reflected in the night
where there sometimes were
fireflies, blurred by the wind
meeting tall grasses
sharp, delicate scars

like bees flying out of her mouth

what does an indian look like, anyway?

basil johnston

this poem starts with a joke
what do you got when there's
thirty-six métis jammed
into a small room
the joke was told by a status indian
who looks white
he wrote a few books called
funny, you don't look like one
he told the joke to a few other status indians
I wasn't there at the time
being I'm not status

one time I told that
funny, you don't look like one
the only people who sometimes mistake me for an indian
on sight, are my relatives, the mohawk
algonquin and cree
ojibwe and other nish
wabanagii and wyendat
and always white people

not right away, since I look white too
silver hair, blue eyes, fair skin
but when they speak to me
for more talk than it takes
to buy food or coffee
help someone across the street
they know I'm not white

they tell me this sometimes, white people do
what are you anyway, they say
what do you mean, I sometimes ask
it's not the way you talk, they say
not your accent
you just don't fit in, if you know what I mean

you make me feel uncomfortable, scared, they say
you an indian or something

I tell them I'm friendly, and, yes, I'm métis
but most folks, they don't know what that means
and they say, so that's your tribe
after asking me this question
one white guy told me his dad said
indians are no better than dogs
and he believed his dad, of course
poor dogs

so, the punch line of the joke is
one status indian
which is kind of funny and
see, us métis, lots of us are status
part white, part non-status
all of us are full métis, full half-breed, full mixed blood
long before our time

our line started nine months after
the white man arrived
with sheep and horses and kfc
long before 6(1)s and 6(2)s, bill c-31s
and the indian act

this poem ends with a text
6(2) whacha doin
6(0) putting together a poem called
"like bees flying out of her mouth"
that starts with a quote by basil johnston
what does an indian look like, anyway?
6(2) hope her mouth isn't full of honey
6(0) what's left is honey
6(2) does she learn what a bitch the queen bee is
6(0) queen's already dead
6(2) cool, are they no longer colonized
6(0) sright. revolution. even god couldn't save her
6(2) cool bees

her voice like downpour on cement

piyak

I'm driving along a rez road in saddle lake on my way
home from northern alberta. I stop at a store to pee. I'm
very fair skinned. long silver hair. blue eyes. everyone in
the store stiffens right up, scared-like. I hear someone say,
cheeee, what's that white lady doing in the store?

deu

I'm waiting in line to use the photocopy machine
where I teach at mount royal university in calgary. a
white woman asks me what I'm teaching and I tell her
I'm teaching essay writing in the aboriginal education
upgrading project. her eyes grow big and round. she gets
all animated and intimate-like and whispers, *well, don't
expect anything from our native students here. I've taught
them myself and the quality of work is disgusting. just set
your expectations low and you won't set yourself up for
too much disappointment.* I tell her, I've been working
there for quite a while now, and I love it. I'm a métis, I
start to say. her voice grows high and shrill, *oh, I'm so
sorry to hear that!* she says, and runs out of the room.

nioókska

just this morning I travel through the blackfoot exhibition
at the glenbow museum in downtown calgary. when I get
a call on my cell from a friend who is fevery and migrainy
and sick to her stomach all day, I start to pace around and
around on the little roads, looking for the way out, in order
to talk in a more secluded spot. I finally stop trying and
plant myself in front of a yellowing, semi-transparent plexi-
glass wall. at first I'm not aware of what's displayed behind
the glass. when I pull my eyes into focus, what I see is a
buffalo hide story robe. I check the black & white photo to
the left and at the bottom of the display that reads, "wolf
collar." I tell my friend, you're not going to believe this. I'm
standing right in front of your great-grandfather's story
robe. it's so beautiful. have you seen it? she says, *no, but my
cousin has given me a copy of the write-up brochure done
by the museum.*

whiteout: an essayic poem

one: introduction and thesis statement

    today was my fourth visit to a museum. I don't like them.
never have. I think of them as one of the great imperialist
institutions, a place of grandiose display and imaginary
conquest, attempted genocide and outrageous white collar
theft.

    by the time I get out of that museum – being forced by the
path to walk through a replica of jacques cartier's mother
ship – I feel like I've been flatlined on the road, like the
crow I catch on my cell phone camera at the tail end of
a down draft. before taking flight again, the crow says,
did you know the formula for cement was lost in a war
sometime in the early-european medieval period, and was
revived again just in time to build things like museums and
schools and the first roads in canada? by this time I'm in
my car, and as the highways intersect with the medicine
wheels, I come to a question asked many times in essays
and in children's books at white rock and white lake
and white river, white meadow, big white ski resort and
big white town, white village, blanc-sablon, and all over
whiter canada. they all want to know, who's the fairest in
the land? I'd lost track of my hands-free in the down-draft,
but I hear the crow yell down,
why, snow white, isn't it?

    snow is cold
snow is white
snow will kill you
in the middle of the night

    whites silence
and our sweet mother
is preparing herself
to destroy

thank god for global warming
no one can escape convention
in-complete sentences and so on
ah, but these are just the facts
you can't believe everything you read

two: body and conclusion

thank the lord for the essay. these are the exact words on
my first text message. then about two texts later, someone
gets carried away with the first six months free and the
digits just grow from there, kind of like weendigo, like
ogopogo or wayzhigwanaad, like the water spirits of
the rivers great and small, but different. if essay were a
character out of greek myth, says the next text message,
what do you suppose he would look like?

probably he would be in the shape of a keyhole. if you put
your eye up to the hole, you can see everything that goes
on inside the room in two dimensions, like a victorian
novel or even a painting. hard on the eye and bad for
the posture, but boring and fascinating at the same time.
everything else blocked out. like pain only different.

> those white guys
> they're all from the
> greek background,
> isn't it, aristotle
> and plato and those
> guys, zeus, adam
> shakespeare and
> stephen king

no two snowflakes are the same
can that really be true

white is right

white's just okay
whites will kill you
in the middle of the day
it's important to believe everything you read

take the essay
bend over and put just one of your eyes up to it
your right eye so it can go into your left hemisphere
make yourself as comfortable as possible
given the squatted knees and the kinked neck
now, stay there for twenty-five hundred years
to ensure obedience
we will bind your body just so
and, of course, we'll have to gag you
but feel free
after five minutes you will begin to perspire
and you will be unbearably cramped
but don't move
remain perfectly still
you will probably soil yourself
and you will probably urinate after a couple of hours or so
but don't move
you won't be able to anyway
and don't open your left eye
if you do
you will see that the walls around you have fallen away
as have your clothes
you will see that the surface upon which you squat
is just larger than the space
required by your feet
but don't worry
you can always put your other eye out

THE HAZARDS OF 50'S LOVE

women loving women is as natural as smiling at a new born baby. that writing brings healing close, ma petite, that writing brings healing close. *great-great granny, exilda dufort-dubois dit lafrance*

first light

is it possible to write
on a scrap of paper, a folding leaf
inscribed inside a rhyme
how sadness feels

it's like trying to find words
for the yellow sound
of wind in grass
a music thirsty
like the sun

or a child
looking back
from a mirror
seeing the future
through the hole made
by that first front tooth

I want it to be tomorrow
when I wash the dishes
I want my kids and grandkids
the cats and the fish

I want to remember
the quesnel river humming bird
who made my ear a flower
lingering, deafening
beak deep inside my ear

seeking the nectar there
a rosehip, red hover
so loud, so long
bringing me the gift
of story

a delicate strength of voice

i) like a paper doll

narrow roads filled with people
heat, hearts, maples, pines
sidewalks, pouring into the sea
makes me homesick
this land that breathes the life
of past loves

knobby knees, walking away
that one, with my hair
frozen to her hem
looks so good from behind
the sound of her voice
the way the rocks make their way
up, up from the centre
back into the fire

is profound, that sound
of river in the air
hard to hold onto during a storm
birds that sing inside the blues
of walls and windows
their day time voices
comforting so many unshed tears

or winter's chill
warming new life
open to the wind
every artery, every ventricle
injured, misplaced
seeking the trees and grasses
the thunder-filled knowings

today I heard that all the
medicine wheels around the world
form a great serpent
bursting out from my own thirst
opening my eyes to hope
or maybe something less cold
to the touch

ii) words blowing the plane around

the bottom of an ocean
all over the land
a river meandering along the edges
of the sand, prairie grasses
cottonwoods, whose dark
black bark leans
around snake skins

as the years pass
my fears dissolve
like powder underfoot
my steps, guided by centuries
I am silenced
by the love

from within these spaces
those places where the ancestors
gather to sing, a shape
in the distance
a great bear meeting, speaking
the stories, their teardrops

I look down at these mountains
blessed by a million questions
as I move into the years
before my reentry into the spirit world
and I know
I don't want to be
another woman's source

iii) nikiy nistohteman kikwaye ahkam itiwek ikwa

I don't understand
what you're saying any more
says a woman in a dream
a woman who holds
another woman's heart
warm and beating
all the openings like red grass
swaying in a wind
that never dies, never stops

she is talking to snakes, that woman
she is remembering
in cree, remembering means
being with only what we can be
rejoicing, calling up those
emotions, memories, senses
spirits, taking that space in time
there, around the edges of living stone
a home gathered by the snakes
from the mountains

she remembers
even ordinary snakes
are messengers
who can't bear to see her
looking at them
she who is inside
another woman's heart
while words have their way
of living, long after the breath

or the sound wind makes
when passing through cottonwoods
through bone
because in her softness

in her greenness, she is very close
and though the speaking is done
through the eyes of those snakes
she is older now, and seeks solitude

love is very powerful
she hears those snakes say
only after she knows the heart in her hands
is her own
only after she knows
there is a stillness on her face
that makes them less afraid
love is very powerful
she hears those snakes say
and has the power to revive people
from the dead

iv) **of tracking marrow to bone**

says she saw a tv show
the other day
a woman from the past
comes round, referred to
as a ghost

even when it's warm
autumn's in the air
thin water pulled out
taking up less space
like any body language

shiny black bellies
swimming upward
pain is
all
all the way home, she says

go home and pray
for the woman
you want in your life
your prayers
will be strong
after the lodge
make your prayers
simple and exact

but my prayer time
interrupted and uneven
eyes inches away
from a large wooden door
a vicious dog
on the other side

boring, lunging, eating
hardwood, eating beech
maybe a roogaroo
teeth biting into
my unfed fear
a small frightened woman
and yet

echoes from the pathway
so powerful
she uses only water
bathes and prays four days
and brings me back to life

v) the power of (un)certainty

you are a mature woman. you've done your work. the way your
light shines onto others, the way others shine in your light, you
could, you should be with someone more like yourself.
lushanya echeverria

like a sadness of not wanting to go deeper
than the surface of a pond
the star blanket of my past, shadows across

the night, when the world is new, I watch the snow
me, not a tree, more a lake, I would have to
walk all the way around myself, but

always come back, like the geese come back
filled with sky's water, drinking from the soil
after centuries of prayer along the shorelines, inside

rock, snake skins left in holes rounded out by rain
or under an overhang, where wind's signature
heard among mud-carved nests, steals into

my dreams, created by wind's touch, fingers circled by
an outstretched palm, hollowed out by ancestral
lines, I'm of the mind that all marks on a page are

magic, settling down and around somewhere between
a scent or the sound of memory, a comma left to blow
or pull at the frayed edges of clean streets, smoothed by

the roundness of walls, my orange smile showing through
like fibres of firelight, lit and facing north, waiting
weaving a story so tender, so bold, so outrageously still

without need, like a desire deep within, my heart
moving me, calling me forward, while day on day
rocking me back to the cradle, my spirit wanting both

subject: re: a snowy november day

on my way to work
thought I'd email you first
feel awful this morning
took two midol but
I'm shaky, don't feel
like being here at all

kitstikakumim, you know
this is my favorite kind of day
where people can split
and lie to themselves
one side to the other
maybe this is part of the fear thing
the old ones tell us about

you're too out for me, you
I feel a sharp rock
growing bigger and bigger
until it blocks my throat
making it difficult to swallow

there's nothing new
under the sun
waiting for the water to rise
lots of people live their lives
as lies
comfortably too
fresh smelling sheets
long nights of reading before bed

I feel like vomiting too
have a game tonight and really don't
feel up to playing
am I nagging
nag, nag, nag

so I love you, more than any woman
I ever have, so what
you're too out for me
lots of women love other women
but they're not out there like you are
can't be with you, can't
oh well, I guess that's what happens
when you're on the moontime
just help me make it thru this day

once the truth comes, it continues
like the rain, the hail
I'm sure my heart has been hit
because I hurt so bad
like silence forcing its way
through old stone

now I smell the scent about me
moontime blood under
the soles of my feet
as if I were a bumblebee
in early spring, hovering
well, that's all for today
good-bye forever
mutsuwapaki

flowers frozen to the snow

woke up this morning in the middle
of a dream, saw crows perched in a tree
in that dream
be careful, sang those crows
be sure your heart's inside your head today

my lover next to me, sleep inside her
she, who has not seen
the edge of life
yet, our bond, eyes, bodies, touch
family, friends, food

years of easy days, of trust
the childhood stuff I shared, she said
in this same wintery bed
don't buy it, sorry, love
your life's like a b-rate tv flick
maybe your truth at the time, but
it's not like they got any blood on them
never been caught

not really hurting anyone, you
but you need help, she said
over a long period of time
undo what was done in therapy
false memories implanted
deep inside your mind

I listened to those wintery crows
told her, no, not my mind
sometimes I'm looking up words
and they don't mean
what I mean for them to mean
but the dictionary says the heart
is the seat of emotion
and me, my heart holds unspeakable

stream of conscious thought
straddles the other side
of sight, of sound, of touch and feel
my own knowing, a slight of hand

by the end of that snowy day
I was single

how is it that white snow on deep, deep blue
can meet with the eyes and become
a window into the future
where winter's cold, the promise of new life
first my children's, now my grandchildren's tiny hands
placing themselves around
my memories, touching through to
the heart I was given at birth

two-spirit love poem, one

if I were to say
in so many words
the newness of water
under your skin

I'd say
there's a path
in the mountains
fenced in by trees
called butterfly alley
flowers chilled by the air
their reds bold
against the greens

or on the water there
behind the trees
where dragonflies
startle the wind
their bodies
rare and bright
their reflections
pooling in the sand

and you say to me
you want to make love
a dream
brushing up against
our hair our lips
our hearts
bursting through
our laughter
into song

two-spirit love poem, two

a light behind your eyes
transforming dreams
with hinges and doors
one evening's melody
moon's slivered light
a song from the past

whose branches
bared of their leaves
dance to the rhythm
forceful winds
of times to come

I hear my name
on those winds
calling me home
where mother earth
opens her womb
for prayer and rebirth

her pulling us up
from the ground
mother earth's mound
ready for snow
her late fall grasses
yellow with hope

two-spirit love poem, three

in some cultures
when a woman dreams
she's sun's lover
she becomes a sundancer

I've had no such
dreams of sun
but dreams of you
as we walk
the blue mountains
winter's sun
warming the sides
of our faces
the backs of our necks

you and me
opening pathways
in the snow
our future
as new to us now
as alive and certain

as the distant
morning star
welcoming sun
as she rises
her face opened
in our eyes

and the sound of her own breathing were in harmony

p.s. today is a good day. you made chili. your daughter loves you. your son is smoking thinking about you. there is one from your past wishing you nothing but love and happiness. there is snow somewhere that remembers the girl in you laughing and precious... and there is a wolf running that saw you once and remembers you and your students think of you when they need help and you have friends who are your family now and you made chili. today is a good day. you made chili. baby steps... just think of all those crees.... ha ha!

richard van camp

today, winter-spring fog, alive
a drive through frozen air
where even the animals are frost covered
buffalo, horses, dark inside white
halos their bodies, open like warm
blackened eyes, see into a world of white
grasses, trees, sky, mountains
oil drills, fences, windmills, peace

yesterday, I should still be there, walking
liquid air in white pines, maples, firs
the shoulder of a mountain
her deep, brown ground still coating my feet
and, oh, I heard so much there, learned so
much in such a short period of time
no wonder the hawk
has such a presence, her voice
her wings reaching, touching

tomorrow, I am trying to write out this pain
ease the ache
in my chest, push at the feelings
like wind coaxes sleet from the trees
their early spring bark exposed in
patches between branches

that air there, bearing
ice droplets, each with its own melody
leaving parts of myself here on the plains
this land where sky and earth intertwine

now, how will I be without her
only nine months, the length
of a full-term pregnancy, when a lifetime
has grown inside a woman's womb
has grown inside my heart
a bird flies over the road
a hawk, baby spiders all around
weaving, reminding me I'm not alone

love rice

I love u
she texts in the middle of the afternoon
while I'm cooking chicken fried rice
and watching over my girl

my girl who's in premature labour
twenty-seven weeks along, too soon
for baby ariston, who moves around in ultrasound
so small and looks like mazie, like daddy

I tell my kids, eh
I tell them what she says
she says she loves me
and I feel so good

I make that chicken fried rice
with so much love
baby mazie can't get enough
love rice, my girl calls it

then that night she tells me, she says
I made a mistake
I shouldn't have said that
I shouldn't have said I love you
I don't

but her love is still in that rice
with mine
still in the chicken, the garlic
in my girl's fridge

not a mistake
a healing meal for a family
who've been through so much fear
holding on to hope
brought home through the hands of love

holding back

there's something burning here
a fire behind my eyes
inside my belly
along the length of my spine

a sea inside my tears
reaching out to grandmother moon
through my heart
the drum of mother earth

beating with desire
to reach that place of stillness
along the red horizon
at day's end

how to hold onto fear
without falling
how to hold onto trust
without fear

there's something small and delicate
pushing up from the land
meeting my face with her hand
a crocus in late spring

and under her warmth
I can feel you
buried and alive
thriving

a mourning song

I find it more desirable to keep a peaceful spirit within me as opposed to an angry or bitter or mean or revengeful spirit. not that I haven't known those spirits. to be able to relate the spirit of peace around me helps me to remember where it came from. this comes from a long line of me.

kenneth little hawk

I tell her, I'm almost sixty
I keep a peaceful spirit
within me, and still
I miss her
in my bed
I close my eyes and I can
feel her in my wrists
behind my eyes
not a bear or a buffalo
or the fenced-in wolf of her dreams

but more a bird
not a large bird
not a single bird
but a flock of small birds

father, mother, family
a small, round nest
things that might embarrass her
being she's a butch

flits from high to low
anger to mean
a birdbath
poof, gone, wind under leaf

washes down the drain
each staging, each je ne sais pas quoi
each joy and glee and flee
for the high, the rush

a flock of small birds, whose young
have been sucked from their shells
their unbroken, empty eggs
mottled and cold
only to find, all yellow and green
a hopeful sadness, settled and caged
her calm heart dressed in a skin of rage

betrayal

despite my age/ I was willing to believe in the magic of deft
hands/ I was willing to believe a woman could be sawed in
half/ and still walk off stage/ so, let's not call it anything but/
betrayal

marilyn dumont

me, I'm done with feeling like
a doormat
heart-shaped stones
leading in, leading out
shadows buzzing in the walls
bumblebees nesting
building sun inside
surround a home so warm
go slow, those bumblebees
hum through the cracks
take in the full moon light
we hold the secrets of life, us bees

I want to keep you all to myself
while you're here, she says
don't want to share you
then in our love bed
can't stand your smell
repulsive, floppy arms, your skin
like the old ladies
where I work

I really like this, she says
I'm not going anywhere
don't want anyone else
hate your ugly, bizarre glasses
wish you weren't here
oh no, no facebook for you
don't have a mean bone
in my body

it's just how I am
it's how my family teases
might grow to like your body
wishing my ex, not you
was in our bed

I love you, I love you, no, no
no, she says, only I can say that
you, you I'd marry
oh, I changed my mind
I may never fall in love

me, I'm done with feeling like
a baseball
in mid-bat
love roses drying on a wall
pushed from her throat in paper words
glass cut with that tongue of hers
bleeding on the snow

IN THE FACE OF WATER

we, the métis, are today, what all of the people on planet earth will eventually become. we are a mirror into the future of the peoples in the creation stories of the world. we are the living spirit and reality of the prophecy of the seven fires.

tánt kelley

prayer ribbons in the trees

the night of first thunders, I walked through the rare wet
air in the bow river valley. there was a shrill cry from a
bird, high in the firs. I tried to make out what kind of bird
that could be, but it was too dark to see that whiskeyjack,
its mate close by, their panic reaching into me. a great
horned owl flew across my path at my waist, up onto a
nearby branch. the owl stayed a while – large fingers and
hands pointing down at me – then took flight, brushing
my hair between me and the trees.

my mom was grandma joan
grandma joan had large fingers and hands
and though she'd plucked and gutted manys a bird
with her large fingers and hands
she was petrified of birds
big or small
owls most of all

grandma joan's large fingers and hands
worked three jobs
filled small brown bags with candy
brought some home when she could
filled glasses with beer and brandy
at the only bar around
took the little ones with her
tucked them under the shelves
next to the bottles of beer
her fingers moving slowly
bead to bead to bead
hail mary full of grace

or joanie dancing
her large fingers and hands
suddenly limber, tender
the pedals of daisies

her black-eyed suzie eyes
whose flowers grace her grave
when winter gives way
to an open-mouthed sky
as nokomis moon slivers, silver

an owl-shaped cloud leaning into the wind
me in girlhood with grandma joan
her eye the moon
in her room
humming songs of solitude
and better times ahead
under the yellow wallpaper
reaching out from its own pink leaves
large fingers and hands intertwined with mine

grandma joan's date squares

1 and three quarters cups rolled oats
1 and one half cups flour
1 cup brown sugar
3/4 cups butter
1/4 teaspoon baking soda
mix rolled oats and sugar thoroughly. mix in well, soda, flour
and butter.

filling: 1 cup white sugar
1/2 pound dates
1/2 cup water
put 3/4 of crumbs in greased pan. add dates. put remaining
crumbs on top. bake at 350 for 25-30 minutes.

her ears no longer speak to her

last night I have a dream where I'm standing inside a house looking out a large plate glass window with my mother. it's early spring. I'm young – dark hair still – and my mom is young too. I'm aware I'm dreaming and through the plate glass window I'm watching myself in another dream within this dream. the other dream is long and I've been helping people reach some kind of destination. I'm not aware that my mom and I are watching from inside the window as I approach the house and start up the walkway. I say to my mom, oh, here I come towards the door. my mom tells me, you can't be in two places at once and I say to her, well, right now I am. I feel good in the dream. happy and content. she says it again, you can't be in two places at once, dear. the dream ends as I begin to open the door, sky wide open.

some nights, in my little girl sleep, bear would break through the plate glass window of my childhood home, warning me of danger downstairs, and I'd wake my sisters just long enough for all five of us to crawl in together and huddle, safe from beer-breathed men who made their way to our bed, us not fooled by their innocent obsession for finding the can.

truth be known, the can was at the top of the stairs – well-lit, door wide open. we'd made sure of that, us five little girls, grabbing our baby brothers before running to the farthest side of the hall and the safety of our big sister's bed. there, we'd hope and we'd pray for a night out of harm's way.

next day, who knew
what or who we'd find in the can
and cleanup downstairs had better be done
before the adults were out of their beds
whatever beer there was left on the walls

or the floors or between the doors
all the empty brown bottles, all the bottles half full
had to be poured into a jar

this would be on a weekend
maybe friday
maybe saturday
maybe both
maybe there'd be two quart jars of beer
by after mass on sunday
or after the hair of the dog

the beer was saved that way
and after supper saturday night, like clockwork
out came the halo shampoo
and one by one we'd kneel on a stool
over the kitchen sink
grandma joan washing our hair
then adding some beer from a cup
keeps your hair rich and full, she'd say
if she had some, she'd use rain water too
keeps the bitter smell of the beer at bay

on other days, much better days
she'd send us out in the rain
go on, she'd say, go on out there, eh
youse kids go on out in the rain
and while you're playing there
you thank that rain
for all that beautiful hair
lining her five girls up on wooden stools
braiding our beautiful hair
that beautiful hair the shiniest hair
in the whole darn catholic church

with the growth of her girls grew a longing
that simple change on a little girl's face
busy traffic from room to room
the voices of many children
whose laughter still lingered
locked inside a love
inside couch cushions, the boston ferns
the browns of each bottle of beer

hummingbirds at the windows

grandma joan never drove. usually she was a white-
knuckled passenger – used to driving with my dad. unlike
grandma joan, I love to drive and when she drove with me,
she'd say, you're a good driver, dear, which meant, take
me to k-mart. grandma joan loved to shop, but not me,
so manys a time I sat in the car and read and wrote and
looked at the sky.

one warm december day, window wide open in the k-mart
x-mas rush, I realized that the chinook arch in the sky
looked more than alive. more than perfect. more than
timeless. that the blue of that sky was the answer to any
question ever asked.

I tell this to grandma joan and she tells me, yes. me and
your dad are going to buy a half duplex. I'm in my fifties
now, she says, and we're going to buy our first home at
last, up that foothill there, the one that reaches out to the
prairie sky. grandma joan spent her last months in that new
house, chinooks blowing through her back yard.

chinooks that revealed patches of blue
caught under yellow grass
where a december sun
pushed out, spreading uneven glows
along the edges of the snow

grandma joan left us during the first real blizzard of
winter, pulling out from underneath a chinook. driving to
the hospital that final day was like being inside a three-d
video game, young couples running across streets together
in an oddly romantic way, still in short sleeves, their dark
shadows, first filling them, then emptying the streets.

and there I was, driving in my car
the blizzard all around me
feeling empty, yet feeling
the spaces between the snowflakes
swollen with hope
with stories from the ancestors
and the smell of date squares
mixed with roasted apple pie

grandma joan baked most friday nights. starting right
after work, she'd line up the aluminum pie plates, dates
for date squares, sometimes cookies or cakes. pudding
or fudge. she'd pour herself some beer in a small glass,
no foam. never poured all the beer out at once. never ate
while drinking. fed us kids, but never herself. held that
glass of beer like granny held her cigarette – all delicate
and dainty and pinky poised like a fine cup of tea.

grandma joan was a slow baker, her large fingers and
hands moving from oven to table, sink to stove, fridge
to beer glass. little turquoise radio on low. I liked to be
around her when she baked and she'd let me do things
– that's how she'd say it – I'll let you peel these apples.
I'll let you pit these dates. I'll let you do this or that
really meant, do this or that, or else. and don't burn that
pudding, waste all that milk. don't overcook that fudge or
I'll tan your hide.

for a while, the house filled with warm, wonderful smells.
then grandma joan'd start to change, her eyes slowly
filling with rage. my mommy was gone, emptied of herself
and her large fingers and hands full of flour and spices
and sugar and song were suddenly weapons of hate.

yet, by the next friday, the bruises faded to yellows.
memory of pain, like the memory of childbirth, faded too,
and when grandma joan lined up the lard and the flour and
her first glass of beer, there I was right beside her, eager to
please.

grandma joan decidedly did not want to die. she fought her
death till the moment she left – not because she was afraid
or because she was angry, but because she truly felt she'd
just begun to live.

grandma joan is going east
she tells me before she goes
east to our homeland, our ancestors in the pines
east with the deer spirits
whose tender moments with their young
in the sun, and grandma joan's hopes
that each of us would remember her
should we meet with deer

east to the place where mary lives
whose virgin blues glowing
beside grandma joan's bed
and inside her yellow eyes
east to that place where jesus lives
her father in the sky

when trees reach up from the water

my first baby was born out of wedlock. that was the popular expression of the day, making him known as a bastard.

the first thing I did was I went to my grandmothers. I was afraid to tell my mom. because grandma joan was fostered out and lived during her teens with my father's sister, I went to my irish grandmother first, being she was my mother's final foster grandmother. I thought about that a lot as a kid – that grandma joan and I shared the same grandmother, who was also her mother-in-law. I wondered, did that make my dad's mom my mother-in-law too? I didn't know my irish grandmother well, but where was a girl to go? when I met with her in her kitchen that day, she told me, glory be to god and mary and joseph too. babies are a blessing and any baby born is meant to be. your mother will be fine – you'll see.

then I went to my métis granny. she was thrilled. she put on a pot of tea. brought out some lemon pudding and tea biscuits. she laughed and said, oh, ma petite, you'll be making these biscuits soon. babies love them, you see. these things are meant to be. don't be ashamed and hold up your head no matter what anyone says. how you feel affects that child. love her, caress her, sing to her, talk soft to her so she'll come into this world in a good way.

I can tell you about myself, she said, that your great grandparents were wed in the rectory because of me. I was in great granny's belly three months already and that was the turn of the century. there's no shame in getting pregnant, ma petite, and if your mother is upset you remember, our babies choose us and not the other way around. our babies are only loaned to us for a time. be happy and rejoice for that new life.

so then I told my mother. she was not happy. she was not gentle. she was not thrilled. the first thing she said was, don't you dare tell your grandmothers.

grandma joan's apple pie filling

1/2 cup white and brown sugar
pinch of salt
1 tablespoon corn starch
1/2 teaspoon cinnamon
1/4 teaspoon nutmeg

mix with cut up mcintosh apples and put in shell. top
with dabs of butter and cinnamon, then top crust. bake
at 450 for 10 minutes, then 350 for up to an hour in all.

rhythm methods and watery melodies

sour apples for pie
plucked from a tree far from the farmhouse
under the tree, a blanket
a cover in the wind, sweet solitude
of an afternoon alone

there, young joanie dancing
her dress swirling high
both knees beautiful still
and love in her eyes

ten years later, young still
and ducks on the water
the blue on their backs shining out
from her seven little children
through grandma joan's dark eyes
their circles pooling
laughter from the beach

there would be days like that, days when hearing laughter
from around the kitchen table meant a game of euchre
or crib and danger was as far away as the beach and the
ducks and the heat.

but children can measure neither time nor distance and
how could I have known that for a teen, a half hour's
walk was all it'd take to reach the sand and trees that led
to that welcoming beach and the warm august waters of
the ottawa? how could I have known that throughout
my teens I'd spend my years sitting at the kitchen table
helping grandma joan with schoolwork so different from
my own? her upgrading elementary through high school
and on to business college while I juggled her learning
and my own? I even learned shorthand, which I promptly
replaced with the sweet scent of love in my eyes.

and the sweet scent swelled with my first born, graham. walked to the hospital with my suitcase in hand – happy and excited. the hospital was french and catholic and the nuns tried to make me wear an old tin ring on the wedding finger, so I made like I couldn't understand french. but they knew I could and they called me madame this and madame that, as if that would wed me in time.

my labour was induced. the baby's head was too big, the doctor said, and I walked the halls, clinging to handles and bright lights and facing the pain on my own. nurses changed shifts three times before my baby was born and a nurse took him away while the sweet smell of life was as fresh as the memory of my own birth, his body my heart. I wanted to breast feed, I told her, and she made like she didn't understand english and told me, go to sleep. rest. in french. and then in english brought a bottle and formula after baby was wiped down and dressed and wrapped. we had no visitors all the days we were there. I called my aunty when baby was born and went back to my bed to sleep.

it took grandma joan a long time to warm up to graham. adored him once she warmed up, but she was bound and determined I'd do it on my own. you chose this path, she said. now live with it.

thing is, I loved my new path and life with my baby. a prouder mom couldn't exist and what I really wanted was to share my joy. yes, when he was born he looked like a cross between diefenbaker and mr. magoo and, yes, his head was very large, but me, I took bus rides in the city just to face him out from my belly so's old ladies could coo and caw at him. I'd sit on park benches and front steps and go down the street house by house, only later learning that's not really how things are done in the city. my boy was born while the thunder reached down from snow

clouds and onto this place that was unfamiliar to us – a city.
we'd grown to know one another in a quieter place.

but, there we were nonetheless and we didn't stay long
in that city. I'd been at carleton, on a scholarship, culture
shocked and taking math, the days before computers and a
single mom couldn't get a student loan in ontario. could in
alberta, though.

back about the time I started helping grandma joan with her
homework – when I was twelve or thirteen – I learned about
chinooks in school. I was both fascinated and didn't believe
it for a minute. so, up we packed, me and my five-month
old baby boy, and moved to calgary. wasn't there two weeks
when I found I couldn't get a student loan for two years.

and though I longed for my homeland
for water and bear and sand
there's a breathlessness about the prairie
that opened up my life
like a basket of sweet red apples
under a late summer tree
the dark of my hair
against the bark of the green of the tree

kihewe watches over us

there's a way a mother has a life planned out for her babies
before they're born – not exact plans or anything like that, but
plans. so when baby is taken, by miscarriage or abortion or
sudden death, it's so important to grieve that baby's loss.
germaine proulx-boyce

seamless stitching on a patch of cloth
blankets for baby
generations of peace, of restful moments
among women and girls
old ladies and young
mothers and daughters
and even the sons
their colours mixing them up with the land
seasons leaving behind
memories of song and laughter
tears and tea, well into the night

there's a place I walk and sit to look down at the river,
my hands all sticky with sap. it's a place I return to time
and again and this is the place I sat after I found out I
was pregnant for the seventh time. I was excited. nervous
and excited. I'd had one beautiful healthy baby boy. one
abortion and four miscarriages, and knowing my aunty'd
had eight miscarriages – and five healthy boys – lifted my
spirits.

I walked that path and sat on the roots of that ancient tree
until early fall and when the leaves began to yellow, that
baby decided it was time to come into this world. I didn't
have time to do much else but get myself to a hospital after
waking up one morning with thick, sticky discharge. not
the pleasant smell of blood and amniotic fluid, but a rancid
smell I knew was not good, not meant for baby.

120

I was twenty-six weeks along, thin and sickly looking. after arriving at the hospital, everything got fuzzy. I'd driven myself there and I was surprised at how quickly things changed, how quickly I changed. I became incoherent and faded in and out of consciousness and I was then transferred to another hospital, a hospital for premature babies.

at the premature baby hospital they'd moved us to intensive care – me and baby still one. told me through a fog of peace and calm, I might not make it. that baby wouldn't be a live birth. the head is too small, they kept saying, and an ultrasound would be a waste of time. I told them, look at daddy's head, there. it's lovely and small. baby's going to be fine. I can feel it in my heart. a mother knows these things. he just needs to come out into this world and get out of the infection that's poisoning us both.

they waited two more days, me and baby growing worse and worse. my first baby, graham – six years old now, knowing he might lose his mommy. panic in his eyes and someone pulling him away.

that night, a night of rain
the trees wet with knowings
me, in dream, hands sticky with sap
finding shade there from the rain
under that old grandmother tree
my back warming her bark
her bark healing my heart
my broken heart
my broken heart
my heart broken

I was alone when I birthed baby deep into the night. there
was one resident, one nurse. the resident was sick all down
his pant legs from the smell of the infection and after he cut
the cord and held baby out from his belly, the silence in the
room overwhelmed me. no green-baby code had been called
– not even a pink – just a young man running from the
room with my living, thriving, air-starved baby. baby steven
didn't stay on this side past eight days. lack of oxygen at
birth, is what they said.

his warmth through his blanket is always on my forearms
– changing my other children's clothes, changing my
grandkids' clothes. hugging everyone in my world.

he looked at me, my baby did
and he told me a dream
about the ancestors
I no longer remember
and I knew this level of grief
must be what it's like
to be alone

baby blankets waiting in a drawer
clean and fresh and holding themselves
one last moment
one last feast
to send baby home

her sleep, her dreams still in her speech

I had a hysterectomy at twenty-six. on april fools day.
I had to go in the night before and I woke up the next
morning with a little stuffed dog by my ice chip cup. the
dog looked like a coyote and said something like, thought
it was your birthday, eh? well, the weather's going to
change and you'd better head for the hills before you lose
count of your marbles.

it was a while before I realized I was dreaming or in and
out of a drug-induced fog and when I did wake up, the
little stuffed dog was gone but her eyes were still there,
hovering next to the ice chips. I ignored them and got up
to pee.

their yellow eyes
like the yellow of their lives
settling on the backs of the hills
their voices magnified
by their songs
ancient and profound
and their songs, always
always
far
too short

try writing that kind of silence onto a page, said those eyes
as I was rolled to the operating room that day.

before the hysterectomy, I'd gone through five months
of constant illness after baby steven was born. d&c after
three months – placenta left behind. staph infection on
top of the one I already had and my womb got eaten from
the inside out. my body formed myself around my bones

and as the infection faded and the colour returned to my
life, there I sat in a hospital room on april fools morning
– coyote's eyes still on me – all drugged and waiting for a
room full of masked strangers to make me into an old lady.

empty spaces between the words
their longing for another time
another moment alone
inside blood and bones
and odours of my own
four moontimes
hush little baby
grandmother's
wisdom's
song

I was reminded of a time long before. by twenty-six,
lying on that hospital bed, I felt old – certainly older than
twenty-one, when I was faced with the decision to end a
pregnancy.

the funny thing was, everything started up on april fools
that time too. a woman I'd worked with was getting
married – out of town and chinooking. warm. sunny, and
a brother of hers who thought I looked like a dream come
true. my dark hair. my blue eyes.

I don't remember what he looked like, but when he invited
me into the back of his stationwagon, the sun shining in on
us like honey and dew – after years of no sex, what could
a young woman do?

a couple weeks later, a strange man showed up where
I worked. stood at the counter and bellowed out my
name between his blonde moustache and beard and
before I reached the counter he said, we believe you have

contracted gonorrhea and we'll need the names of all your sexual partners for the past six months. right in front of everyone – in front of the old scottish ladies I worked with – ladies in their fifties!

no one spoke to me about it. not me or anyone else. I simply walked through the returning cold and snow – every lunch hour – the sixteen blocks, then back, to press a button twice for venereal disease and I waited my turn for a needle in the butt the size of a juice glass. days down the road I encountered my first penicillin-fertile yeast infection.

movement in my belly
holding on to life
with a touch so soft
so tender

creator's tiniest babes
whose sacrifices
grandmothering manys a young woman
into blossoms
grieving their losses
alone

as spring unfolded herself around my womb, I found out I was carrying another child, my fertile body's simple joy forming her features into my pores, my body's odour a flower waiting to open around herself in the middle of a tree.

but none of this was meant to be. there were complications. there were signs and a d&c was ordered and there I sat in a hospital room remembering april fools afternoon and a chinook arch that pulled the prairie to the depths of my me.

had grandma joan known she may have disowned me. but I
didn't tell her. I couldn't, and she ended up nursing me. she
knew I'd had a d&c, like the others I'd have down the road,
but an abortion?

and coyote was right there on the bed
her yellow eyes resting on the edge
of my pillow
licking the salt from my tears

a comic irony, she said
as grandma joan brought tea biscuits and tea
and changed the pillow case
under my grief-stained and watery head

grandma joan's tea biscuits

2 cups flour
3 teaspoons baking powder
pinch of salt
4 tablespoons cold shortening
3/4 cups milk

mix together dry ingredients. knead in shortening on board, using as little flour as possible. roll out 1/2 inch thick and cut with floured upside down glass or biscuit cutter. bake at 450 for 12 minutes or until golden brown.

tiny spruce and thunderbird eggs

birds whose voices open patterns in the trees
their yellows and greens and red-tipped wings
settling like pollen on the ground
filling the pathways through the trees
with echoes of their songs

last night I dream of three birds, each of them a replica of
the next. the first is a small songbird who flies into the house
through the open door. the bird is colourful, her feathers a
crazy quilt of brilliant yellows and reds, oranges and greens,
purples and blues.

grandma joan is in the next room, cornbread baking, her
fear of birds frozen in her floury arms. so, though I long
to listen longer to the songbird's song, I lead that baby
bird back out through the open door. no sooner does that
songbird leave than in walks a prairie hen looking like she's
quilled and quilted with the same splashes of colour, her
wings wiggling and her bottom bouncing as she makes her
way towards the kitchen – her toes click-clicking on the
linoleum floor.

then barb walks in the door. barb, who travelled twice the
distance to be with me, her black hair thick and delicate, her
round crown circling her perfect tiny head, her hands the
flutter of butterflies, flying through town to announce her
birth. brother held her first, his little boy wings brushing,
touching her face, her hair, her hands. the look in his eyes
– a knowing from the spirit world – reflected into mine as
he passed his sister in a breeze so gentle, his scent her sweet
protection, for life.

barb's my baby still, now with children of her own. in the dream she tells me, mom, don't put that bird outside. I saved her from the zoo. but the bird is gone and framed in the doorway – the sunshine bright against the deepest reaches of a chinook arch – is my little tweety-girl, my granddaughter jessinia, holding a small stuffed crazy-quilted bird.

look, nokomis, look, she says. I got her at the zoo. her name is great grandma joan and she likes corn bread and fresh, hot tea. and up comes a wind only the prairie can bring, sand rushing through the open door like fog over water.

sand in my throat
songs that coax the ancient ones
to their homeland
and still, after all these years
that moment I looked into barb's eyes
her looking into mine
I knew she knew me too
then jessinia, born eyes wide open
hers looking into mine

we three are
trees inside the rain
each round drop
surrounded by the sound
of mother

grandma joan's corn bread

1 cup yellow cornmeal
1/2 cup flour
1 teaspoon salt
1/2 teaspoon baking soda
1 tablespoon baking powder
1/4 cup (or so) sugar
1 cup buttermilk
1/2 cup milk
1 egg, beaten
1/2 cup corn oil

preheat oven to 450. grease muffin tin or 8 by 8 pan. pace in oven about 3 minutes. combine first 6 ingredients and mix well. add last 4 and mix well. turn oven down to 350 and bake about 20 minutes or until golden brown.

and the monarchs are up before it's fully light

a cree elder once told me, when you're small, time goes by nice and slow. then when you grow up, time flies by. but then when you start to get old, time slows down again. I sure hope that's true.

their childhoods rushing by
like a southerly wind, fragrant
and warm and welcoming

barb was born when the summer was greeting the fall and throughout her childhood years, every leaf she drew was yellow. barb, whose role in my life exceeds all other roles – the bond between mother and daughter a multifaceted and multilayered kaleidoscope, like one of those toys we had as children, looking down the tube and into the light at an unlimited number of colour-filled shapes and surprises.

her tender touch on my back
her tiny hands, hot
knowing the language of my skin
her skin and mine, the largest organs in our bodies
facing one another and in our hold
hearing the words sculpted there, deep
into our pours

and now my grandchildren. willow, jessinia, and even mazie, only five months old, born eyes wide open and looking into mine. already she knows this language, carrying her wisdom from the spirit world into her baby seat, into the bath tub, her change table, onto the kitchen floor.

grandma joan watches over them
the four directions of the medicine wheel
bringing balance and growth to our bond
and there are times when we are one thought, one heart

generations of children, playing
holding a moment's laughter
out into the night
dew drops forming around their mouths
their lips, sweet, melting harmonies
taking up room inside each others' lyrics
each others' songs, abounding in
little by little
whatever words wind blows to their ears
they listen, they are
monarchs, migrating into view

Credits

"Inside the Depths of Dark Water: Heartwords of a Métis Lesbian," chapter, including poems, "the one shaped like a winter leaf," "spiders," "a delicate strength of voice: like a paper doll, words blowing the plane around, nikiy nistohteman kikwaye ahkam itiwekikwa, of tracking marrow to bone, the power of (un) certainty." *Indigenous Women's Knowledge.* Eds. Nicole Lugusi et al. University of Alberta and McGill University, 2012.

"e s a r i n t u l o m d p c f b/ v h g j q z y x k w," Feb-May, 2011. "a world of red," *Our times: Canada's Independent Labour Magazine,* Jun-Sep, 2011.

"spiders." *Strength and Struggle: Perspectives from First Nations, Inuit and Métis Peoples in Canada.* Eds. Rachael A Mishenene and Dr. Pamela Rose Toulouse. Toronto: McGraw-Hill Ryerson, 2011.

"spiders," *Yellow Medicine Review: A Journal of Indigenous Literature, Art and Thought. The Ancestors We Have Been Looking for We Have Become: International Queer Indigenous Voices.* Fall, 2010.

"rhythm methods and watery melodies," "her sleep, her dreams still in her speech," *Exile: The Literary Quarterly.* Vol. 32, No. 4, 2009.

"her voice like downpour on cement: a pentagon," *West Coast Line, Special Issue: Citizenship and Cultural Belonging,* Vol. 43, No. 3, 2008.

"tiny spruce and thunderbird eggs," "her sleep, her dreams still in her speech," "rhythm methods and watery melodies," *Journal for the Association of Research on Mothering,* Vol. 9, No 2, 2007.

ACKNOWLEDGMENTS

I would like to begin by thanking the mysteries, the ancestors, for my life and my family. I am grateful to the peoples of Treaty Seven for so lovingly caretaking and graciously sharing this land with those of us who now live here. And I humbly honour Kainai First Nation multi-media artist, Joane Cardinal-Schubert (1942-2009), who touched so many. Of her work, she said, "So many stories are in each work, they are not just my story, they are the stories of all the people that are a part of me – those that formed me by their actions so many years ago, my teachers, my colleagues, and my family." Her favorite childhood memory was of a walk she took on the land with her father when she was four years old. He said, "You have to be so careful as every footstep you take will change all things."

Like Joane Cardinal-Schubert, my stories and poems are not just my own, but part of all the people who are a part of me. My children, Graham Angus and Barb Horsefall. My son-in-law, Harold Horsefall, and his mom, Valerie. My grandkids, Willow Eagle Speaker, Jessinia, Mazie and Ariston Horsefall. You all fill my life with pure joy. My aunty, Evelyn, who's my inspiration and my light and her twin, Catherine, together with uncle Jacques, thank you for your constant love. Always, my sister, my good friend, Joy. Adrian, you're still close, even when you're far. My late mom, Jeanne d'arc Marguerite and my dad, Ed. My sisters, Faye and Anne, my brothers, Ed and Phil and my late sister, Gail. My nieces, Aimée, Tanya, Megan, Abbie, Dawn, Ti-Anne, Fawn. My nephews, Trevor, Kurstyn, Philip, Jason, Eddie, Chris, and all your children, youse are all inside me, eh?

My good friends, Margie Faccini-Lee, Amina Dawed-Baker, Aruna Srivastava, Weyman Chan, Renée Lang, Clô Laurencelle, Amanda Ribbonleg-Mills, Fritz Bitz, Lisa Harris, Gale Blondeau-Getz, Carla Osborne, Rhonda West, Joe White, Doreen Kallies-Lamirande, Sandy Smokeyday, Christine M. Goodwin, Robin Kirk, Shannon Kopf, Jeffery Brazeau. Even when we don't see a lot of each other, you're all so close to my heart. Cindy Deschenes and Amanda Ribbonleg-Mills, for sharing your stories. Lushanya Echeverria and Kim Bittner, and Bonnie Fabian, for offering me a quiet, beautiful place to write, on Camel's Hump mountain in Vermont and in the breathless mountains of North Vancouver.

Before I sit down to write, I smudge and light a candle to honour the grandmothers and grandfathers who help me. Because quite a bit of my writing also comes from the grandmothers in my dreams and it is made clear to me what dreams are meant for my writing, I keep a diary. Not that I record my dreams as such, but keeping a diary keeps me fresh. There are times when a poem will come in its whole and I make no changes. There are times when a poem or a paragraph or a story will take literally years. The good news is, I always seem to know when they are done.

All of the titles for my books have birthed themselves from dreams except this one. *The trees are still bending south*, comes from my good friend, Margie Faccini-Lee. We were driving one late spring day a couple of years ago. We'd planned to go for a walk, but it was really windy so we decided to take a drive instead. At one point she said, "the trees are still bending south." Such a poignant, stunning description of this land where I've lived for the past thirty-eight years. I am from the ottawa river valley, where the odauwau zeepih, ktchisipi – her waters wide as a lake – meets with the abeed waewae zeepih, the petawawa river. I come from dynamic Algonquin land and I now live on equally dynamic Blackfoot land. We are related, us. I had no idea these wor(l)ds would become the title of this book. Thank you, Margie.

My biggest influences are Native writers and storytellers. Still are. Too many to list. E. Pauline Johnson, Louis Riel, Beth Brant, Paula Gunn Allen, Basil Johnston, Rita Joe, Jeannette Armstrong, Susan Beaver, Chrystos, Beverly Little Thunder, Marilyn Dumont, Louise Halfe, Richard Van Camp, my friends Joanne Arnott, Connie Fife, Greg Scofield and Weyman Chan – are some of my many heroes. Shirley Bear has reached into my bones with her visual art and her voice. She is one of the great thinkers of our time. Daniel David Moses is a man whose poetry and theatre challenges my every writerly fibre. Lee Maracle has unraveled and created theories of writing that have helped me to find my own voice. Marie Annharte Baker's voice is one I've held close to my heart almost all my adult life. Linda Hogan is the author right now that I most admire. To me, her writing is absolutely brilliant. From Maria Campbell – besides being the first Métis writer I ever read – I learned to rewrite the queen's english in a real and self-aware way that challenges the white, male norm. From Emma LaRocque, the second Métis writer I read, I learned to love myself for who I am. From Luce Irigary, a french feminist writer from france, I learned my womanness can be expressed in english in an entirely unique way. And from Susan Sontag, a Jewish american political activist, I learned the beauty of the mind when the heart is woven in. I acknowledge my debt to all the writers I quote and mention in these pages; their words are integral to these poems.

My thanks to Daphne Marlatt, who encouraged me to start publishing in 1990.

Certainly not last, I would like to thank Kateri Akiwenzie-Damm and Renee Abram. I am in awe of the work you do, the way you turn books of poetry into works of art all over again, each so lovingly brought into print for a new audience.

Every moment in life is a prayer. Myself, I not only embrace poetry as a form of prayer, but also as a form of resistance. In the autobiographical poems, "forty thousand feet," and "you can see that lake in the sky," I ask, "am I a poet, then, am I working/ to make change, to speak out our spirits/ help us know what we must do?" I am of the mind that the artists, the writers, the musicians, those in theatre and entertainment – not only comment on life, but provide a means to change. Louis Riel predicted today's movement. As Shirley Bear reminds us more than twenty years ago in, *Changers: A Spiritual Renaissance*, and again in 2006 in, *Virgin Bones: Belayak Kcikug'nas'ikn'ug*, "Artists are the movers and changers of the world. They have always been revolutionaries, creating change in thought and style within their societies. We have no desire to produce work that either looks like or is connected to any European tradition or movement. It is not our way."

CCAC: Forty Voices Decolonizing Cancer

In 1996, my sister, Joy, was diagnosed with stage-four colorectal cancer and given the grimmest of outlooks – seventy-five per cent chance she would die. I was so frightened, and I can only imagine how my sister felt, her with a twelve-year-old son. Joy is still here today – and every day to her is a living miracle. All of us who know her are blessed.

I'm in my fourth year of volunteering with the Colorectal Cancer Association of Canada, also known as the CCAC. We meet yearly in Toronto for training and some of the most dedicated physicians and surgeons in Canada present on the latest medical strides concerning colorectal cancer. Almost all of the forty or so volunteers are survivors of stages-three-and-four colorectal cancer, and, like my sister, most of them were given a death sentence by their doctors. Every year, I am humbled by their stories and infused with the medicine of the dedication – the positive, joyful, insightful atmosphere that dominates the three days. Each of the CCAC volunteers wrote their thoughts on paper in June, 2011, and, because our words were so disparate, I was not yet able to compose a poem called, "the seven sacred directions."

I volunteer at the CCAC to help Native peoples. I am a patient. Colorectal cancer is almost one hundred per cent preventable through colonoscopy. Poof. Gone. Just like that. Most people don't know that. I didn't. And, colorectal cancer is most prevalent among Native and Black peoples.

My sister had stage-four. Our mom died at fifty-four of lung cancer in 1986 and it's now known that the type of lung cancer she had wasn't a primary cancer, but a secondary, more than likely metastasized from colorectal cancer. Colorectal cancer doesn't present symptoms until it's advanced. A simple colonoscopy takes off polyps in the colon that, if left to grow, almost certainly will turn into cancer.

To raise awareness of the importance of screening and colonoscopy for colorectal cancer prevention, the CCAC has a giant colon, they travel from city to city across Canada. My goal as a volunteer at the CCAC is to have the federal and provincial governments and donors, not only sponsor a giant colon that travels from city to city across Canada, but sponsor a team of doctors and nurses who travel colonoscopy equipment to Native peoples in remote communities in this country, instead of merely supplying body bags.